SYSTEMATIC
BIBLIOGRAPHY

SYSTEMATIC BIBLIOGRAPHY

a practical guide to the work of compilation

fourth edition revised by
A M LEWIN ROBINSON
BA PHD FLA

with an additional chapter by
MARGARET LODDER

CLIVE BINGLEY   LONDON

K G SAUR   MUNICH · NEW YORK · PARIS

First published 1979 by Clive Bingley Ltd
Set in 11 on 12 point Baskerville by Allset
Printed and bound in the UK by Redwood Burn Ltd
Trowbridge and Esher
Copyright © 1979 by A M Lewin Robinson
All rights reserved
ISBN 0-85157-289-8

Clive Bingley Ltd
Commonwealth House, New Oxford Street, London WC1

K G Saur Verlag
P O Box 71 10 09, D-8000 Munich 71

K G Saur Publishing Inc
175 Fifth Avenue, New York NY 10010

K G Saur Editeur
38 rue de Bassano, F-75008 Paris

British Library Cataloguing in Publication Data

Robinson, Anthony Meredith Lewin
    Systematic bibliography. — 4th ed.
    1. Bibliography — Theory, methods etc.
    I. Title
    010'.28   Z1001   79-40542

    ISBN 0-85157-289-8

CONTENTS

5

CONTENTS

PREFACE

THIS ATTEMPT at formulating the main principles involved in the practical work of compiling bibliographies results from the belief that no satisfactory guide for the use of students and others inexperienced in bibliographical techniques is readily available. The only publication covering this field would seem to be M V Higgins *Bibliography; a beginner's guide to the making, evaluation and use of bibliographies*, and that treats the subject very briefly. Other works on different aspects of bibliography there are of course in plenty, but these either concern themselves with scholarly bibliographical description, or are general introductions to the subject, devoting little more than a single chapter to systematic method (eg Esdaile). Apart from these there is of course Georg Schneider's monumental *Handbuch der Bibliographie* which, with its English translation, provides an invaluable theoretical and historical analysis, but which is not calculated to appeal or be of practical assistance to the novice of today with a project before him.

This guide then is intended for the non-librarian who is obliged to undertake bibliographical work, as well as the student of librarianship who must acquire a familiarity with bibliographical techniques and be able to apply them. For this reason a list of textbooks is appended which will assist the beginner to acquire some knowledge of the basic procedures of cataloguing, classification and bibliographical description, which are essential to good systematic bibliography, and on which so much has been written that there would be no justification for repetition here.

Methods of reproduction are today so numerous and so rapidly developing that any attempt to include a description

7

of them or of the peculiar problems which many of them present would be of little lasting value. It is therefore left to the bibliographer to seek technical advice on these questions. The increasing importance of the computer to systematic bibliography however has obliged us to include an additional chapter on computer applications by a specialist in this field, Miss N M Lodder of the Centre for Scientific and Technical Information, Council for Scientific and Industrial Research, Pretoria, to whom I am most grateful.

The illustrations, gleaned from some of the finest examples of contemporary bibliography, are by no means the least part of the book and the author gratefully acknowledges the sources from which they are taken.

A M L R

1

THE MEANING OF BIBLIOGRAPHY AND ITS VARIED FORMS

THE TERM 'bibliography' has a very wide connotation for the English-speaking student or scholar, covering the whole field of the science of books as physical entities—their history and changing forms, the materials and methods of their construction, their description and recording in lists. Leading bibliographers differ slightly in the names they assign to the various branches of the subject. Esdaile and others divide it into three:

1 *analytical* (comprising the detailed analysis of the structure of the book and its description);

2 *historical* (embracing the history of the various methods of book production, including printing and adornment); and

3 *systematic*, which may be preliminarily defined as 'the preparation of lists of books'—in short the compilation of bibliographies.

W W Greg, supported by Theodore Besterman, combines analytical and historical under the one head 'critical,' but all are agreed on 'systematic.' Greg actually regards this as the only true bibliography, the systematic application being mere drudgery and prostitution of learning. In this he is not supported by Besterman nor by A W Pollard and Sir Stephen Gaselee (see *The library* fourth series 11 1931 241-262; 13 1932 113-143, 225-258). There is an obvious distinction between the historical and analytical branches of the study of bibliography, but they both belong to a science capable of lending itself to pure scholarship; systematic bibliography on the other hand is an art or technique dependent much upon their application. The three (or two) branches are naturally much interrelated. The learned bibliographer may be, and has often been, able to assist the literary scholar in the establishment of the authenticity of his text or the chronological order of varying versions, by purely bibliographical deduction from the manner in which the book is bound up or from the paper on which it is printed, proving of invaluable assistance to textual criticism. Such research can be simply of an ad hoc nature, but of how much greater service to scholarship will it be if the result, recorded according to certain generally recognised rules, is carefully and systematically arranged with others, to form a bibliography.

All bibliography of course is not on this high level of scholarship.

It is imperative that one should be quite clear about this distinction at the outset, because outside the English-speaking world—and among certain American bibliographers as well—the question does not arise for the reason that by 'bibliography' or its equivalent is understood only that part of the subject which we have called systematic, ie its application to the compiling of bibliographies. The rest is described as the book sciences, the book arts (German. *Bücherkünde*) or even by that unpleasant word 'bibliology'.

If this difference of interpretation is appreciated we shall be able to consider some of the several definitions of bibliography suggested by world authorities to help us arrive at a fuller comprehension of our subject, of which we have so far given a most inadequate definition. The word bibliography will henceforward be used in its internationally accepted sense and not in its wider English one.

The very brief definition we have used above—'the preparation of lists of books'—is that of Georg Schneider in his *Handbuch der Bibliographie*, and a work which, while still unique and very important, contains much that is both confusing and unnecessary for the beginner in bibliography. His definition is inadequate in that it stipulates no principle or order of arrangement of the lists to be prepared, nor any special degree of selection or description of the books in them. A mere list of authors and titles issued by a bookseller or publisher for purposes of advertisement is not a bibliography, nor on the other hand is a library catalogue, however full its entries may be or however well classified, though some few approach it.

10

The UNESCO/Library of Congress bibliographical survey *Bibliographical services; their present state and possibilities of improvement* by V W Clapp (Washington DC, 1950) expanded the definition to: 'The technique of systematically producing descriptive lists of written or published records'. This is more satisfactory as it emphasises the essential need of system and description and indicates the inclusion of other material than books. It still however does not suggest any fundamental difference between bibliography and the compilation of library catalogues. This difference of course lies in the fact that the catalogue is concerned with the contents of a single library or group of libraries and describes only the copies of books to be found therein. A bibliography is not so confined, either as to the location of the material it records nor to the description of the particular copy of each work which the library chances to possess. The bibliographer in fact, is concerned with the whole vast product of men's minds on paper, wherever he can lay his hands on it, for his aim is not to guide the seeker to the contents of one collection, but to help him to find his way about in that great sea of literature which increases so alarmingly year by year, either by simply answering the question 'What has been written' that can help me on the subject?' or, the often more complex one, 'Which edition or variant of this book is it that I have and does it vary from others?' As we shall find later, there may be much difference between these two approaches to bibliography.

Schneider differentiates them as the academic (in its literal sense, of course) and trade, and the 'bibliophilic,' the imputation being that the first is largely concerned with contemporary literature and is intended for the student, the researcher and the bookseller; while the second, concerned with rare and antiquarian items, is for the collector who wishes to collate his precious acquisitions and establish their identity in case of doubt. In the latter case description will need to be very much more detailed than is required for most contemporary work, and every discoverable variant will be recorded. Here Schneider falls short of actuality, as the scholar and the librarian may well have recourse to the 'bibliophilic' bibliography to identify their copy or to determine which is the earliest text of several.

11

Fredson Bowers in his book *Principles of bibliographical description* defines this class of bibliography as 'descriptive,' and regards it as the only true one. Bibliographies which do not aim to give a definitive account of a book and to record every known variant, he prefers to call 'bibliographical catalogues.' We shall probably not be prepared to accept his whole contention but there is no reason why we should not prefer 'descriptive bibliography' to Schneider's 'bibliophilic.' The other sort, for want of a better name we shall call 'enumerative'. There is of course no clear cut division between the two types and both require a background of scholarship if the work is to be authoritative.

Mlle Malclès formerly of the Sorbonne, in her book *Les sources du travail bibliographique*—a work concerned more with the enumeration of bibliographies than with the techniques employed—describes bibliography as being based upon '*research, identification, description* and *classification* of documents, with a view to organising the services or constructing the tools destined to facilitate intellectual work'. The research part is concerned with the discovery of the material to be included in the bibliography, after which each item must be clearly identified, then described and finally arranged according to some rational principle—ie classified.

In common with many other bibliographers, Mlle Malclès finds it hard to decide whether bibliography of this nature is an art or a science. She comes to the tentative conclusion that the learned variety, which we have decided to call descriptive, approaches a science, while the other (enumerative) is purely a technique. The writer's opinion, as suggested above, is that we are concerned primarily with a technique, but one which demands a thorough grounding in the book sciences plus language and literature. It is interesting to compare Mlle Malclès analysis with that of a great British bibliographer, Sir Stephen Gaselee, who forty-six years ago in 'The aim of bibliography' (*The library* fourth series 13 1932 225-228) divided bibliographical work into five stages: 1 collection, 2 enumeration, 3 description, 4 analysis and 5 conclusion.

Collection, enumeration and description comprise the pure techniques, while analysis and conclusion are the scholarly

12

aspects which approach the scientific and will only feature in descriptive bibliography.

It is hoped that the question of definition has not been unduly laboured since the guide will not primarily be concerned with the scholarly aspects of the subject but rather with its technique. It has been discussed at this length to prevent too narrow a conception and to persuade the scholar that the business of the systematic bibliographer is not merely the drudgery that Dr Greg would have us believe.

From the foregoing exposition the aim as well as the meaning of bibliography has naturally transpired, but to remove any further doubt let us formulate it:

The aim of bibliography as here defined is to assist an enquirer in discovering the existence or determining the identity of books or other documentary material which may be of interest to him.

Clearly this object can only be achieved by appreciating the needs of the hypothetical 'enquirer', as we have called him in preference to the 'student' or 'scholar'. These needs must not be ignored, as it is only too easy to do. Bibliographers may still be met with who believe in bibliography for bibliography's sake, but this point of view is not to be upheld when there is so much important work to be done. Nearly eighty years ago Mr John Ferguson in an otherwise estimable address to the Edinburgh Bibliographical Society entitled *Some aspects of bibliography* (page 32) displayed the perfect academic approach when he exhorted his audience in selecting a subject for a bibliography to pick on anything that came to hand—a street, an individual or an arbitrarily chosen year—with no suggestion of preliminary assessment of its ultimate value. He even advocated as a subject books of a particular size. He likewise pays tribute to the scarcely apposite sentiment of a cynical poet: 'a book's a book, although there's nothing in't' (Byron in *English bards and Scotch reviewers*).

But for us bibliographies must fulfil a need, the field must be chosen with care and the arrangement be that which is most likely to be helpful to the user. Even allowing Mr Ferguson's all-embracing approach to be suspect, the field is enormous, though much is already under control.

The field of bibliography may be divided up as follows:

GENERAL

1 *Universal*: Only a few years ago this was no longer considered practical as a centralised project and the nearest convenient approach to the problem of listing the world's total output of books seemed to be through the published catalogues of the great national libraries such as the British Library (then British Museum), the Bibliothèque Nationale in Paris and the Library of Congress, this last being superseded in 1956 by the publication of the *National Union Catalogue* of the USA. Writing in the *Library Association record* in 1953 (55(6): 178-182) Dr Louis Shores said of the *NUC*: "It is necessary to understand that even its 13 million cards may be eventually the smaller part of a total project which now envisages listing and locating virtually all the records of civilisation whether in books, serial or audiovisual form . . . Possibility of reproduction of the NUC is under consideration, though at high cost, and it may be that here we shall have the nearest approach to universal bibliography." As already stated, the publication of the current NUC began in 1956 while in 1969 there was a further valuable development in the retrospective cumulation of *NUC* with the publication of its *Pre-1956 imprints*, soon to be followed by *1956-1967 imprints*. It is significant however that neither of these very considerable projects is yet complete, though they soon will be.

As far as current universal bibliography is concerned however, valuable as the great national library catalogues will always be, the future unquestionably lies in the application of the computer and in shared cataloguing whereby each country is responsible for the recording according to internationally accepted rules (ISBD) of its own publications, the records being made available by means of MARC (Machine readable catalogue) tapes from which the catalogue entries can be printed out on cards, film, in microform, or simply called up on a video screen. As more and more countries develope their own compatable MARC systems, so will universal current bibliography become more of a reality.

14

Chapter five will explain computer applications more fully.

2 *Language groups*: World bibliographies of books in the more important languages are of trade and library value. The *Cumulative book index* endeavours to do this in English, while its French counterpart *Catalogue de l'édition française*, includes the publications in French of Belgium, Switzerland and elsewhere as well as France with some attempt at completeness.

3 *National*: Many countries have their current national bibliographies produced either commercially or by state institutions. Fine examples are *British national bibliography* and *Das schweizer Buch*, the latter recording Swiss books published in French, German, Italian and Romansh. In Denmark, in addition to the national bibliography, a bibliography is produced of all books locally published in foreign languages (*Dania polyglotta*). This is of some importance in Scandinavian countries where many contributions to knowledge appear in English, French or German in order to reach a wider public. Computer applications in this field have been developed considerably (see chapter five).

4 *Regional*: There are few quotable examples of general regional bibliography covering a group of independent though nevertheless interdependent countries, but in those areas where common problems are becoming increasingly appreciated such a project may well be desirable. A bibliography of this type has already been started in the West Indies under the title of *Current Caribbean bibliography*.

SPECIAL
This division comprises bibliographies of:

1 subjects: eg chemistry, history, geographical areas, famous persons;

2 forms of literature: eg poetry, fiction, drama;

3 books published in definite periods of time: eg incunabula, sixteenth century books;

4 special categories of literature such as: banned books, best sellers, translations, forgeries, books by certain classes of people: eg women, members of a religious order.

All these can be treated from the following points of view:
a) international; b) regional; c) linguistic; d) national; e) of
period in which published.

In addition we have the following special types:

5 the works of individuals, sometimes styled bio-bibliography or author bibliography;

6 the imprints of smaller than national areas: eg provinces, counties, towns, presses:

7 editions and variants of individual works: eg the Bible, the first folio of Shakespeare. These of course may all be treated from the period point of view, and no 7 from the linguistic in the case of books much translated eg English translations of *Don Quixote*.

It is naturally possible to find subjects which fall between these categories and the tabulation is not presumed to be exhaustive. A further division of the field is possible as regards the physical form of the material to be included. This may be in any of the following forms but not necessarily all: 1 printed books and pamphlets; 2 periodicals; 3 articles appearing in periodicals and other composite publications; 4 manuscripts, and to these may nowadays be added 5 films, filmstrips, photographs and television programmes on videotape; 6 gramophone records ('discography') and magnetic tape recordings; 7 posters.

The listing of these audio-visual records by themselves can not be regarded as bibliography, but their inclusion as an appendix to a true bibliography would be acceptable. In like manner purely pictorial matter is outside our scope, though *iconography* may likewise form a useful appendix to the bibliography of any subject.

So much for the division of the field. What of the form in which the bibliography may itself appear? According to the subject it may be either: 1 current—recording contemporary literature as it appears with no termination in view; or 2 retrospective or non-continuous, including for example all books published before or in print on a certain date or in a certain period.

These again may be produced in the following physical forms: a) as books—2 above favours this form; b) as periodicals; c) as items in periodicals—1 above favours these last

16

two forms; d) as a series of lithographed or printed cards for those who want up-to-the-minute information in an easily supplemented form; e) microform, or any other photographic copy; or f) computer tape.

The following chapters will endeavour to show how the problems presented by these many forms and types of bibliography should be tackled. Bibliographies may range from the comprehensive to the highly selective and in detail from the simple check-list (not strictly a bibliography at all) to the work with full standard bibliographical description and considerable annotation. The abstract again is a specialised technique. Except for the introductory chapter, this guide is intended to be eminently practical. The theory and history of bibliography have been dealt with by such authorities as Theodore Besterman in his *Beginnings of systematic bibliography*, Georg Schneider in *Theory and history of bibliography* and Mlle L N Malclès in her *Les sources du travail bibliographique*.

Likewise standard bibliographical description—the method of describing a copy of a book in such detail that it can be identified in its absence without any doubt—is to be found most adequately covered by Cowley *Bibliographical description and cataloguing* (Grafton, 1939), Fredson Bowers *Principles of bibliographical description* (1949) and E W Padwick *Bibliographical method* (Clarke, 1969). Examples of suitable styles will be all that should be necessary and that there can be room for here.

17

2

THE COLLECTION OF MATERIAL AND
THE MECHANICS OF COMPILATION

IT IS TO BE presumed that in most cases the choice of a subject for a projected bibliography will have been predetermined by demand, and to a large degree the form in which it will be issued as well—ie current or retrospective, in book or periodical form etc. Frequency of publication, however, in the case of current bibliographies may only be possible to decide upon when the field has been surveyed and the amount of material suitable for inclusion discovered. To students and others anxious to embark upon useful bibliographical work but with no special mandate, the warning is again issued against the danger of purely academic bibliography and exhortation made to consult the scholar and the scientist, if not the librarian, who may be able and glad to recommend desirable subjects.

Whether the bibliography is to be current or retrospective, the fundamental methods of compilation are the same and most of the same decisions have to be made—indeed it is not uncommon to have a retrospective bibliography supplemented currently. These primary decisions will be:

1 how the field is to be limited;

2 whether the work is to be selective or comprehensive;

3 what forms of material are to be included (eg books, periodical articles etc);

4 what form of entry is to be used.

The answers to these questions will depend upon the subject, its size and the funds at the bibliographer's disposal. In the case of 1, a final decision may not be possible before one has already advanced some way in the compilation and knows what one is up against. The project, for example, may be the bibliography of a large city and its environs. It

19

may be provisionally decided to include all works published up to the year 1980, but should it be discovered that these are very much more numerous than at first imagined, further limitation will be desirable if completion is to be possible within a reasonable time or budget. This can be effected either by reducing the period covered, the area, or omitting certain classes of material, and no general recommendation as to the most desirable is possible. Needless to say the converse—too little material—may also occur and call for widening of the field.

Whatever the subject of a retrospective bibliography, the date must be clearly laid down after which items published are not included. In the case of current bibliographies, published weekly, monthly or whatever it may be, it stands to reason that this closing date will be strictly periodical and predetermined for each issue. The *terminus a quo* is of equal importance.

Decision 2—selection versus comprehensiveness—will largely rest on the size or extensity of the subject. In a small field (200-300 items) selection need hardly be considered unless a reading list only is demanded, but it may safely be said that the larger the field the greater the need for selection though it may not always be practical. If selection is to be made with safety, we must pass from the sphere of the bibliographer to that of the subject specialist. In the realm of science, opinions differ markedly on the question of select bibliography, even though it may be admitted that today it is often impossible to peruse everything written about any subject. So do not be selective unless you are confident you know just what you are about or have the advice of an expert. Purely physical characteristics, such as number of pages, are a dangerous criterion. It may well happen that an article of less than one page contains the first intimation of a discovery of the greatest importance, or the only notice of an historical event. The bibliographer has likewise no right to be biased. Exclusion based on personal prejudice is unpardonable.

There are many bibliographies, needless to say, of which the whole raison d'etre is completeness, and these include: national, author and early printed book bibliographies. In such cases every effort should be made to include everything falling under their respective headings.

Decision 3 is on the forms of material to be included. We have already detailed those possible in chapter 1, namely: a) printed books and pamphlets; b) periodicals; c) articles appearing in periodicals and other publications; d) manuscripts; and possibly films and gramophone records.

Questions of arrangement apart, one would ideally include material in all these forms, but in practice this is not always done. General bibliographies will almost certainly be confined to one form only, ie books, as the mass of periodical articles will be too vast to be conveniently recorded in the same volume. We shall then find only books in national bibliographies, with perhaps the first issues of periodicals, and periodical articles will be covered by *indexes to periodicals*.

With special bibliographies it will depend upon the amount of material presenting itself and the demand for up-to-date service. It has for long been generally appreciated that the rapid advance of science and technology renders publication of current research in periodicals essential as the time lag inevitable with books is too great. No bibliography of an advanced field such as atomic physics or electronics, or even in the biological sciences, can therefore be other than largely composed of periodical references with the addition of the few considered monographs that appear in book form.

On the other hand, in the humanities, though periodical literature has its important place, a geographical area or a period of history may very well be covered by books alone. From its nature, research into topics in these fields is more likely to be published in book form and the scholarly public is prepared to wait—albeit impatiently!—for the appearance of a new theory or piece of criticism in print. If any proof of this is needed, it will be found in the differing character of the 'references' or 'literature cited' at the ends of scientific and of non-scientific works respectively.

One must not, however, generalise too much; bibliographies will be found in the humanities containing periodical articles as well as books, but more often than not the retrospective bibliography will be confined to books and the

21

periodical contributions will appear in current bibliography. In author bibliography, as already stated, it is the compiler's business to assemble everything that has issued from the pen of the subject in order to produce as true a picture as possible of his life's work.

The inclusion of manuscripts is only likely to be an occasional problem. When the location of valuable historical source material, in the form of unpublished documents or private papers, is known it should certainly be recorded in the bibliography of the personage, place, period or movement in history with which it is connected. The form of such material being so different from that of the printed word, however, it will almost certainly demand a separate index or calendar and receive only brief description in the bibliography. Similarly in an author bibliography, or that of the editions of a celebrated work, the location of manuscripts should be recorded if known. Since in the former case they are presumably unique—though not invariably (for example, Robert Burns was in the habit of sending MS copies of his poems to his friends)—there is little point in giving many bibliographical details about them, the principal aim of descriptive bibliography being to assist collation and establish the identity of different printed copies. The scholarly work of comparison and description of ancient and medieval manuscripts is outside the scope of this book.

The fourth and last preliminary decision is the form of entry to be adopted, ie the manner in which the author, title and other details of each item are to be presented. Dealing firstly with full-length books we have at least four possibilities:

1 *Short title* (as in Pollard and Redgrave's *Short title catalogue of English books to 1640*). For example:
    14766 JONSON, BENJAMIN. Every man in his humor. 4º *F. W. Burre*, 1601.

2 *Standard catalogue entry* according to Anglo-American code rules. For example:

GRAHAME, Kenneth, 1859-1932.
The wind in the willows; by Kenneth Grahame.
Illustrations by Arthur Rackham; introd. by
A. A. Milne. London: Methuen, (1950).
xii,[i]), 178p. front., illus., 11 plates, 23½cm.

3 *ISBD* (*International standard bibliographical description*) (Suitable for computerised cataloguing and as used by the BNB.)
GRAHAME, Kenneth
The wind in the willows / by Kenneth Grahame;
illustrations by Arthur Rackham; introduction by
A. A. Milne.– London: Methuen, 1950. – xii, [i],
178p. col ill; 23cm.

When there is more than one volume the pagination of each should be given in a note following the entry: 'v.1: xi, 234p.; v.2: vii, 356p.' This is not library catalogue custom. Another departure in current bibliographies is the noting of the price of the book which may form an integral part of the entry. Yet another variation, favoured particularly by scientists, is the insertion of the year of publication after the author's name (compare plate 18). This is an advantage in bibliographies of research papers where the date of publication is all-important.

4 *Standard bibliographical description* (as used for antiquarian and rare books and first editions; compare Wade's *Bibliography of the writings of W B Yeats* in the Soho bibliographies series, and Gallup's *T S Eliot: a bibliography*, see plates 1 & 2).
GRAHAME, Kenneth. THE WIND IN THE WILLOWS
The Wind in the Willows/BY KENNETH GRAHAME/
[Vignette] /ILLUSTRATIONS BY ARTHUR RACKHAM/
INTRODUCTION BY A. A. MILNE/METHUEN & CO.
LTD. LONDON/30 ESSEX STREET, STRAND, W.C.2.
23½ x 15 cm. xii, 178p. 11 coloured plates including front., headpiece to each chapter. p. [i] Half-title, verso blank; p. [iii], title, on verso: *This book was issued on October 8th, 1908,/since when it has been reprinted in a*

variety of/editions, illustrated and unillustrated, 96 times/
Ninety seventh edition; 1950/Catalogue No. 5326/U/
printed in Great Britain; p. v-vii, Introduction; p. ix,
Contents, verso blank; p. xi-xii, Plates; p. xiii, fly-title;
identical with half-title, verso blank; p. 3-178, text; 1
blank leaf at end.
Issued in dark green cloth lettered in gold on spine:
THE WIND IN THE WILLOWS/Kenneth Grahame/
METHUEN. Cream end-papers; top-edge green to match
boards.
This is the first edition to be illustrated by Arthur Rackham
although it was always the author's wish that he should do
so.
In this example it should be clear that the first paragraph
gives a fairly exact transcription of the title-page while the
second supplies the collation in sufficient detail to make
confusion of editions next to impossible. The third paragraph describes the format and would also include a note on
the size of the edition if this were known, while the last
gives other information of interest about the edition. If the
book were a composite work, a full list of the contents would
follow, though if it consisted of merely a small number of
parts, these could be detailed in the collation. In an author
bibliography, the short title heading, which is included
purely for easy identification, will probably be omitted.

5 *Full standard bibliographical description* (as for early
printed books in the British Museum *Catalogue of books
printed in the XVth century*). For example,

a) PETRARCA, Francesco. Bucolica.

8 January, 1499/1500.

b)   1ᵃ, Title: Bucolica Francisci petrarchi 2ᵃ. (headline)
Parthenias ‖ Viri p̄clarissimi atq3 insignis Francisci
petrar‖che de florētia Rhomæ nup laureati bucolicum ‖
carmen incipit in xij æglogis distinctum. quarū ‖ prima
ītitulatur Parthenias Collocutores autē ‖ Siluius et Moni-
cus ‖‖ [M]Onice trāquillo solᵍ tibi ꝑditᵍ antro Silui ‖ . . .

c)   37ᵃ, l. 25, Colophon: Viri p̄clarissimi atq3 poetæ īsignis
Frācisci pe‖trarchæ de florētia Romæ nup laureati bucolicū
‖ carmē Imp̄ssum Dauētriæ. Anno dñi .M. cccc ‖ xcix.
Octaua Ianuarij.

24

d)   Quarto. a–e⁶ f⁸. 38 leaves, the last blank. 3ª: 27 lines of leaded text and headline, 146 (152)×93 mm. Types: 106 G., title, headings, headlines, colophon; 88 G. Lombards. Capital spaces. Campbell *1384. Hain 12828.

This book is taken to belong to the year 1500 on account of the reintroduction of minuscule a with wide lower loop in 106 G., as in the following Cyprianus, 29 November, 1500.

The text is leaded throughout.

The earlier form of N of type 88 (81) G. is used in this book.

The headlines give the titles of the eclogues.

A blind impression of type 88 G. is distinguishable on 1ª. A similar impression on the same page in the Cambridge University Library copy (ULC 3514) is identifiable as deriving from 7ª (b 1), l. 6 to end, including signature.

196×133 mm. Bound at the British Museum bindery in brown sheep.

Bought in April, 1882.   IA. 47715.

In this example, taken from the British Museum *Catalogue* above mentioned, v.IX, the entry is for an incunabulum printed in Deventer by Richardus Pafraet in January 1500. Paragraph a) (so here described for easy reference) gives the short title and b) gives a transcription of the actual title-page followed by the headline on the recto of leaf 2. c) gives the colophon or concluding paragraph of the book in which details of printing usually appear. d) gives a detailed collation with exact measurements of the printed area, the type used and references to two authorities. Subsequent paragraphs refer to the particular copy examined concluding with the outside measurements. In a bibliography a final paragraph might mention known variants of the book and any other pertinent information.

It has already been pointed out that within the compass of this guide it is impossible to do more than give examples of these different forms of entry as they require books themselves to be treated adequately, and if the would-be bibliographer is not already familiar with them he must by all means make himself so before he can begin work. Recommended textbooks will be listed at the end of this book, though cataloguing is an important subject of study in librarianship courses, and demands much practice.

Of the above, forms 2 and 3 are naturally best suited to ordinary enumerative bibliography. There are many varieties of entry in use beyond the above (see Esdaile's *Student's manual of bibliography*; third revised edition, page 262, for an example of 2 adapted to descriptive bibliography) and latitude is permissible in the actual style. The amount of detail and annotation desirable will depend upon the character of the material and the degree of scholarship demanded by the subject. In chapter 4 the presentation of several different styles will be illustrated and compared; they all, however, contain the same essential information which experience has shown to be most useful.

Example 1 (*short title*) is to be used rarely, as it gives very little information and is suited to a check list rather than a bibliography. One cannot go far wrong with standard library cataloguing (example 2) or ISBD for all general enumerative purposes, as they include all the essential details for the identification of a contemporary volume for everyday purposes, *viz* author's full names, full title save in exceptional circumstances, illustrators, editors, translators, etc, edition, imprint and brief collation.

Bibliographical description is required (examples 4 and 5) when the aim of the bibliography is not simply to give information on what has been written, but to describe works in considerable detail for purposes of comparison and identification by scholars, librarians and collectors. Sometimes the copy to be compared may be imperfect, and without recourse to another, it is necessary to discover how much is missing. More rarely the title-page itself may be wanting and require reconstruction. The categories most likely to receive this attention are those of antiquarian interest such as classics, travel books, early printed books, the products of private or particularly celebrated presses, and also the literary works of individual authors who have achieved an important place in the eyes of scholars and collectors.

The best form of *analytical entry* used for recording periodical articles and those taken from other composite works, such as yearbooks, symposia and *Festschriften*, is that recommended by the Anglo-American code, for example,

McDougall, William
The riddle of heredity. (*In* The forum, New York, v.79, 1928, p.xii-xvi.)

This reference is capable of some abbreviation as long as there is an adequate explanatory key provided. The place of publication may be omitted when it is certain there can be no confusion of two periodicals of the same name, and volumes and pages may be reduced to such expressions as:

34(1): 57-63, D 1936.

Which equals:

Vol 34, pt 1, p 57-63, Dec 1936.

Finally, while it need not actually concern us at this stage of compilation, cognisance should be taken of the international standards for the abbreviation of periodical titles, (See *World list of scientific periodicals*, published in the years 1900-1960, London, Butterworth, fourth edition 1965-66, subsequently taken over and supplemented by the *British union catalogue of periodicals*), for example:

J. Amer. Soc. Agron.=Journal of the American society of agronomy.

The use of these standards is essential for scientific bibliographies today and their users will understand them. In other subjects however they may be less popular.

In reference to composite works other than periodicals, little abbreviation of the title is permissible and the publisher should be given. For example:

Psychical research as a university study. (*In* The case for and against psychical research; ed. by Carl Murchison. Worcester, Mass., Clark University Press, 1927, p. 149-162.)

The form of entry for periodicals as such will depend upon whether they appear incidentally in the bibliography or comprise one by themselves. If the former, they will naturally follow the style prescribed for book entries as much as their format permits. Practice varies much in library catalogues—particularly regarding change of title—and all styles are not suited to bibliographical use. In enumerative bibliography the form below is the simplest to adopt, it being appreciated that added entries under changes of title are not necessary, references being adequate. Entry under the latest title is now most favoured. For example:

The London quarterly of world affairs, v. 1- Apr./June
1935- [London] : Stevens [etc]., 1935—
-v. 18½-25cm.
    Title varies: 1935-Apr. 1943, the New Common-
wealth quarterly; July 1943- The London quarterly of
world affairs.
    Bibliographies of periodicals are not so common as other
forms of literature due to the comparatively small number of
titles, but when they are compiled their intent is usually to
show what periodicals are in progress in given fields, or to
indicate where they are to be found—the latter being really
union catalogues. Examples of these are Ulrich's *Periodicals
directory* and Gregory's *Union list of serials,* or *Periodicals in
South African libraries.* Comparison of their forms of entry
will ullustrate their differences.
  a) *Ulrich*
    CHILD study; a quarterly journal of parent education.
    1923. q. $1.4° Child Study Association, 221 W 57th
    St. New York 19. bibl., bk rev. radio progr. index.
    Indexed: Educ. Abstr. Educ. Ind. Psycho. Abstr.
  b) *Gregory*
    London quarterly of world affairs. London.
    1, Ap/Je 1935+
    1-8. Ap/Je 1935-Ap 1943 as New Commonwealth
    quarterly.
        [Names of holding libraries.]
    Ulrich is concerned only with current periodicals while
Gregory aims to include everything that has survived in
United States libraries, as far as can be ascertained. Consequently, though it is not necessary to give collation in the
former, but only date of establishment, the compiler must
supply details of frequency, price, publisher and address.
Additional notes help the prospective purchaser assess the
value of the publication. Gregory on the other hand must
give details of volume numbering with dates and changes of
title, as the list will not only be used to locate back numbers
but also by librarians and collectors to determine whether
their own files are complete.
    The descriptive bibliography of periodicals is rarely met
with, as each volume—in fact each issue—of a journal is a

bibliographical unit deserving of individual treatment. Few examples of this form of literature are bibliographically interesting for the reason that different editions of a particular issue are only very occasionally found and variants other than those resulting from purely fortuitous binding are rare indeed. (These remarks do not apply to newspapers which frequently have several editions per diem, but it is not suggested that they would form a profitable subject for bibliographical research.) Now and then we come across issues of interest because of suppression in whole or in part, or with supplements that have been lost from most copies. In most cases however, detailed description will be needed largely for the purpose of enumerating the contents, the subject matter being of more interest than physical peculiarities. Only periodicals of considerable rarity will warrant this, such as the 'incunabula' of this form of literature in any part of the world, and others that have become collector's pieces such as those made popular by the researches into Victorian popular fiction of the late Mr Michael Sadleir. Mr Sadleir has presented us with the best example of a form for dealing with rare periodicals in volume 2 of his bibliography of *XIX century fiction*. An example will be found on plate 5. See also examples in Cowley, J D *Bibliographical description and cataloguing*, pp 167-73.

ANNOTATION

Much more than in a library catalogue, from which it is presumed the books are physically not far distant, annotation of some sort is necessary in any compilation with pretensions to the bibliographical, though it may not be needed for every item. As in cataloguing it should be concise, with the omission of all unnecessary verbiage. Notes may be of several kinds and the following are the most common:

1 In elaboration of the title when the subject is insufficiently clearly expressed. For example:

[Title]　　Was Darwin wrong?
[Note]　　Outlines the great schools of evolutionary theory: Lamarckian, Darwinian and Neo-Darwinian.

2 Contents note; for example:

Anderson, J. N. D. *ed.*

The world's religions.

CONTENTS: Animism, by A. T. Houghton—Judaism, by H. D. Leuner—Islam, by J. N. D. Anderson—Hinduism, by G. T. Manley and A. S. Neech . . .

In enumerative bibliography this will be confined to books containing the work of several authors as above, or several distinct works by the same author—collections of poetry and essays excepted.

3 On editions and changes of title—of especial importance in trade bibliographies; for example:

a) [of a 2nd edition] Contains new preface, otherwise unchanged.

b) Evening industrial schools . . . Revised ed.

Originally published as *Adult education: the evening industrial school*, 1930.

4 On relationship to other works; for example:

The group mind; by William McDougall.

A sequel to *An introduction to social psychology* by the same author.

5 Regarding circumstances of writing (particularly in bibliographies of individuals); for example:

The nature of functional disease; by William McDougall.

Annual address before the American medico-psychological association, Boston. May & June 1921.

6 On the qualification of the author—only necessary when this has especial bearing on the subject and its addition considerably enhances the entry's value; for example:

Sparrman, Anders.

A voyage to the Cape of Good Hope, towards the Antarctic Polar Circle and round the world . . . 1785.

The author, a naturalist, accompanied Capt. James Cook on his second voyage.

Such notes may vary from a single line to as much as a dozen in rare cases in enumerative bibliography. When for reasons of space, annotation must be cut to a minimum, 1, 2, and 3 are the most important.

In the case of descriptive bibliography very considerable annotation is only to be expected, and here again the reader must be referred to Cowley and Bowers. The above examples will always be applicable with amplification, since it is the business of literary bibliographies to give as complete a history as possible of each item therein, though not an appraisal. That work of this nature is a specialist's and may demand years of research should be clearly understood. The excellent bibliography of W B Yeats, by Allan Wade (3rd ed Hart-Davis, 1968), for example, is claimed to be the product of fifty years' acquaintaince with the subject, and the author even so admits that it may not be exhaustive (see plate 1). The same applies to the work of Sir Geoffrey Keynes.

Abstracting, ie the summarising of books and periodical articles so as to give the researcher or specialist a clear idea of their contents, is an extension of annotation but not really within the field of bibliography. The handling and arrangement of the finished abstract, however, is. The principles of abstracting will be found clearly explained in such books as the Bureau of Abstracting's *Principles of abstracting* (Brochure no 4, 1948). An example of a bibliography with annotation approaching the abstract form will be found on plate 18.

As many of the above questions as possible should be settled by the compiler before starting the collection of material, as it will save much time and labour if entries do not have to be radically altered when work is well under way. The arrangement of the bibliography can and may often be planned in advance, but in no event should one feel bound to adhere to any preconceived scheme if the material when collected suggests modification of it.

COLLECTION OF MATERIAL
The mechanics of collection and preliminary recording of material demand media that can be easily handled and arranged. For enumerative bibliography most workers will find standard 5 in x 3 in (12.7 x 7.6 cm) catalogue cards most suitable, though slips are undoubtedly cheaper and may be an economic necessity for current bibliographies using hundreds a month. The normal procedure is for each

'master' entry for inclusion to be entered on a separate card or slip, the latter to be arranged in the way that will be most beneficial to the user and necessary guide cards added for section headings etc. If the bibliography is to appear in typewritten or mimeographed form the master slips may be in manuscript and typing done only once. If, however, it is to be printed, the cards should be typewritten and type set up from them or photolithographic plates made from them as is frequently done. Except in the rarer cases where a bibliography is preserved in card form, it is obvious that the necessary life of the master card or slip is very short compared with that of the library catalogue card, but the handling of a stiff card is in many ways more satsifactory than thin paper and leads to less chance of entries being overlooked or misfiled.

National bibliographies often adopt the practice of recording each item first on a slip suitably laid out according to the form agreed upon, with all the invariable parts of the entry printed. These invariables include all the possible features of the collation, eg: 'p., illus., plate(s), tab(s)., diag(s)., ... cm.' etc. Much time is saved by simply ticking or adding numbers to these items and the entry is exceedingly clear for the typist to copy on to cards. This is only worth while for current bibliographies making hundreds of entries a month, or for centres producing a succession of retrospective bibliographies, as does the Swiss National Library. It is naturally useless for descriptive bibliography where the length of each entry is likely to vary greatly.

The actual search for material should be pursued in as methodical a manner as possible. It has long been the dictum of authorities in this field that 'the honour of the bibliographer' obliges him to glean from first hand sources and not to depend on secondary ones. In other words he must personally examine every item included in his bibliography and not depend upon the work of others, ie publishers' and trade lists, printed library catalogues and other bibliographies. There is always the chance that these may have errors, in which case he will be merely repeating them. If this ideal seems sometimes impossible of attainment, as it may, the bibliographer must clearly admit his fall from grace by distinguishing the unseen items by an asterisk or some such sign, and stating his authority for the details supplied.

There are numerous possibilities open when collecting titles for most bibliographies, setting aside national and other general ones which must be dependent on the accessions of legal deposit libraries or on special arrangement with publishers.

(As a matter of interest the following are the methods for collecting materials adopted by some national bibliographies: a) British national bibliography—legal deposit; b) Belgium—legal deposit; c) Canada—formerly arrangement with publishers, now legal deposit; d) Denmark—arrangement with publishers, though there is legal deposit; e) Holland—commercial venture; f) South Africa—legal deposit; g) Switzerland—arrangement with publishers.)

Taking retrospective bibliographies first, the following are the most likely sources for titles—a preliminary to the search for the actual books themselves. They are given in the probable order in which they will receive attention:

1 *The catalogue of a large general library,* or

2 *The catalogue of a special library* of the subject under consideration.

These can be combed to form a nucleus for the work in hand, whether subject or author and in case of really large projects photographic reproduction is to be recommended.

In most cases such catalogues will be a guide to books only, though some special libraries maintain an exhaustive index to pertinent periodicals. When this is lacking—or indeed to supplement it—assuming that periodical articles are to be included, resort must be made to:

3 *Periodicals covering the field*—if such exist. The labour of search will generally be lightened by consultation of the published indexes to periodicals, such as the *Readers' guide to periodical literature, Social sciences index,* the *British humanities index,* and *Internationale Bibliographie der Zeitschriftenliteratur.* More specialised indexes include the *Applied science and technology index,* the *Art index* and the *Biological and agricultural index,* while in the more highly scientific and technical sphere, abstracts form the equivalent of periodical indexes, eg *Chemical abstracts* and *British*

biological abstracts, and in the social sciences and the humanities we have *Current sociology, Education abstracts* and the like. All these may yield a fresh crop of items for inclusion, which must be traced and examined.

The location of periodical holdings in many countries may nowadays be determined with the help of union catalogues, such as the *World list of scientific periodicals* (Great Britain), the *Union list of serials* (USA), the *British union catalogue of periodicals (BUCOP)*, the *London Union list of periodicals* (libraries in London), or *Periodicals in South African libraries.* All these indicate in which libraries the periodicals listed in them may be found.

Continuing with the sources of possible titles, we next have:

4 *National bibliographies* and other general lists, such as the *Cumulative book index, Catalogue de l'édition française, Brinkman* (Netherlands) and *Deutsche Bibliographie,* if arranged by subject, or even if not for author bibliographies.

5 *Bibliographies of bibliographies* which will direct one to:

6 *Other special bibliographies* in the same or related fields. The bibliographer need not think that the existence of a bibliography of a subject already necessarily renders further work in that direction valueless. Augmentation and improvement is often possible either with respect to currency or method of arrangement. It may well be that bibliographies in related fields may give one considerable help. If, for example, the subject were PUBLIC FINANCE it might be that a bibliography of BANKING would contain useful items. It is impossible to eliminate all overlap between bibliographies just as it is impossible to draw a strict line between subjects of study.

7 *Published library and union catalogues* both general and special. The value of the British Museum (Library) *General catalogue of printed books* and the US *National union catalog* as the nearest approach today to retrospective universal bibliography has already been stressed. Unfortunately the subject indexes of the first (preceded by Peddie's *Subject index to books to 1880*) appear only every five years while the second only started issuing a subject catalogue

34

in 1950. Many other libraries such as the London Library, the Royal Commonwealth Society Library and the Royal Institute of British Architects' Library have published printed catalogues of great value. These will be found recorded by Besterman in *World bibliography of bibliographies* (Geneva, fourth edition 1965-66).

8 *Bibliographies in books.* Most treatises on a subject, if of a high standard, include bibliographies or lists of references, either at the end of each chapter or at the end of the book. Sometimes, as in the case of the *Cambridge history of the British Empire*, these are considerable and specially compiled apart from the text. Even if they are a mere afterthought, or a brief record of the works consulted by the author while writing the book and of doubtful accuracy, they may be useful.

9 *Reviews* etc. Many specialist periodicals publish a book review section regularly. Routine examination should be made of these. In the case of author bibliographies when it is desired to include reviews of the author's work, search may be made in the issues of periodicals most likely to give authoritative criticism for a few months following date of publication of the original work. The best sources of course facilitate matters with indexes listing reviews under a separate heading. For others the periodical indexes mentioned under 3 will help.

10 *Trade catalogues* other than the general ones mentioned in 4. These include publishers' and booksellers' catalogues, often issued in a broadly classed form or covering special fields only, eg Francis Edwards' *Africana* catalogues and Sotheran's *Bibliotheca Chemico-mathematica*.

11 *The catalogues of any library* one may chance to visit. Generally one will be visiting libraries with the bibliography particularly in mind, but it should become second nature to take every opportunity.

It is a good plan to keep a record of all sources consulted for future reference, but particularly so in the case of periodicals which have proved fruitful, so that they may be regularly examined.

Contemporaneously, and as the result of searching the foregoing secondary sources, the bibliographer will be seeking the books and other items themselves. Aids such as union catalogues have already been mentioned. In addition, inter-library loan services will have to be used to the utmost. Even taking full advantage of these, however, travel is almost inevitable, unless one intends to confine oneself to a biblio-graphy declared to be limited to material in the libraries of a particular centre, which is hardly a bibliography in the strict sense of the word. Even working in London, it may be found that a visit to Oxford or Edinburgh is necessary to ferret out a work not available elsewhere or to visit a special collection, and with descriptive bibliography this is likely to be even more essential than with enumerative.

The assistance of workers in other centres is the next best thing to going oneself, and the development of photographic reproduction has been a great boon to bibliographers as well as other researchers. The acquisition of photocopies of essential pages, such as titles, colophons and variants, will do much to uphold 'the honour of the bibliographer' at little cost! The writer, in Cape Town, has had to supply such facsimiles to bibliographers of law at the Hague and of Australiana in Melbourne.

Where rare books are concerned, it is more desirable to record in the bibliography itself a selection of the libraries or private collections in which copies have been located. This greatly increases the value of the work for the student, but renders it desirable for the compiler to track down copies of each book in different parts of the country so that a geo-graphically spread selection may be offered. In the case of Pollard and Redgrave's *Short title catalogue* and its supple-ment by Wing, this constitutes one of its major functions since the bibliographical information given is of the very briefest. The locations are usually recorded in abbreviated form, with the city or town indicated first, eg LM=London, British Museum; OB=Oxford, Bodleian Library; WF=Wash-ington (DC), Folger Library.

Assistance from other centres may of course be planned as co-operative effort and many admirable compilations have resulted from such work. This will be further discussed below.

As the name implies, and by definition in chapter 1, current bibliography aims at recording periodically the current output of the printing press, as soon as possible, it may be assumed, after publication. While in some restricted fields this can be achieved by a single individual (compare *Index medicus danicus,* compiled for years in Copenhagen by *one* member of the University library staff, but even he had his work carefully checked by others), it is more likely to require the co-operative effort of several persons under an editor-in-chief, each covering a portion of the field or the analysing of a certain set of periodicals. Obviously such activity must be very carefully planned at the outset and will continue as strict routine, the same fruitful sources of material being regularly examined, while a roving eye is ever on the lookout for untried sources. These sources will differ from those helpful to retrospective bibliography in obvious ways, though much of what has been recommended above will still hold good. It is now the accessions lists rather than the basic catalogues of libraries which must be consulted, the current issues only of the national bibliographies, the indexes to periodicals and the periodicals themselves.

In current work, though there must inevitably be some delay between the publication of a book or periodical article and its appearance in a bibliography, to reduce this delay to a minimum the compilers must chiefly be dependent on what is currently received at the centre in which they work. Obviously no such project should be contemplated divorced from an adequate documentation centre maintained either by legal deposit, purchase or arrangement with publishers for 'review' purposes.

Any officially recognised current bibliography will probably come to some agreement with the publishers who stand to benefit by the inclusion of their titles. There is no time for the compilers to indulge in lengthy correspondence regarding the accuracy of entries or to travel about seeking material. If all the material in a field cannot be received at one centre then a degree of punctuality must inevitably be sacrificed. There is no reason however why the co-operation of several centres should not produce a satisfactory result if a clear standard form of entry is adopted and the various contributions give evidence that they are well capable of applying it correctly so that the editor is not obliged to re-do most of the work. The more contributors there are, the greater chance of error and delay there will be. Straightforward bibliography will not experience such a delay but the human element must be taken into account. It will do no harm to re-emphasise here that *accuracy is one of the most important attributes of the bibliographer.*

Bibliographical work is frequently associated with the cataloguing departments of large libraries. When this is so it will usually be found that labour-saving devices have been evolved whereby the work of the one assists the other. A most striking example of this may be seen in the Swiss National Library in Bern, where accessions are first catalogued on a master slip as described above, page 31, at one side of which there is a column of abbreviations representing the various bibliographies currently maintained. A tick against one of these indicates that the entry is to be considered for that bibliography and a card will be made for it and sent to the respective editor, whose initial work is thus much reduced. It may be noted that automation has not yet been introduced here though most of the bibliographical data in *Das Schweizer Buch* is included in MARC. Similar economies can be effected in bibliographical centres unattached to a library, as for example the Bibliotekscentralen in Copenhagen. This office produces a national bibliography, numerous book selection guides and catalogues of children's books, as well as running a card service for public libraries— all with the minimum duplication of effort. It may also be remarked here that the BNB, while not originally produced in the British Library, has always been compiled from the books received by the agent for the copyright libraries.

Before leaving this subject, what may be described as the 'scissors and paste' method should be noticed. This is the cutting up of printed catalogues, accessions lists etc from different sources and mounting the slips on cards. Many scientists and other specialists keep their own card bibliographies for private use in this manner, and a number of learned societies issue an index slip with each number of their journal intended for the purpose just described. For a personal file it is highly satisfactory, but the lack of uniformity among entries added to the dependence on secondary sources renders the method unwise for the accumulation of entries for a published bibliography.

Where the scissors and paste method will be found invaluable is in the preparation of revisions of retrospective bibliographies. Obviously it will be desirable to revise most bibliographies after a period of years to incorporate new material, but it is naturally not to be expected that the revision will be based on standing type after that time. In any case changed outlook may have made it advisable to alter the whole system of arrangement, eg from subject-classed to classified (see chapter 3), or the method of production, to a computerised one, (see chapter 5).

Whether the original bibliography has been supplemented periodically, occasionally, or not at all, the same principles will be involved in preparing the revision, and the original will be the basis on which we must build. To make this practical the entries must be transferred to cards, a comparatively simple process if two disposable copies of the original are available. After a preliminary check for any items to be excluded, these copies may be cut up and the entries mounted on 5 in x 3 in cards (used ones if need be)—the scissors and paste method. This work can be done quickly and easily by means of photographic dry mounting tissue which lies between the copy and the card and is fixed by means of a hot iron—an operation not requiring the supervision of a trained bibliographer. Supplements can of course be treated in like manner and cards can be rearranged, corrected and added to as required. If the basic work and supplements have been printed or typed uniformly and not too much manuscript correction has been necessary, it is feasible that the rearranged cards might be reproduced by the photolitho-offset process at a very much lower cost than printing (compare *National union catalog*). Usually however for clarity retyping will be desirable, preferably on an electric machine.

In the event of two copies not being available for cutting up, as may well be, a photographic copy should be obtained for mounting in a similar way, as the expense and time involved will still be less than that of typing out the original.

CUMULATIONS

Cumulations are the result of the merging or intercalation of the entries of two or more issues of a current bibliography so as to form one. The intent is to save time spent in consulting several issues. This re-arrangement will not of course upset the original plan of the bibliography. How often it may be done depends on the size and frequency of appearance of the work and varies greatly. Some few cumulations are, like the weekly BNB, progressive, ie the first four months of the year are cumulated, then the first eight, and finally an annual volume appears with perhaps a five-yearly cumulated index. The H W Wilson Co's *Cumulative book index* is now published monthly, except August, every third issue being a cumulation of the two preceding ones.

Small lists may only require cumulation annually.

There is little likelihood nowadays of cumulations being produced by traditional printing methods such as linotype composition requiring additional entries to be dropped into the standing type, as used to be the practice. Rather the same photolithographic method as recommended for revisions on the previous page will be employed. Cards can be easily preserved so that new items can be inserted and the augmented copy rearranged and rephotographed. All this can be done in the editorial office without the danger of printers' errors. Opportunity however should be taken to proof-read and correct any errors that may have become apparent since publication of the earlier issues.

INDEXES

The making of indexes will be discussed towards the end of the next chapter, but one aspect of it is not out of place here. Every bibliography worthy of the name needs an index and it is possible and advantageous in many cases to make index entries concurrently with the main entries. This makes for greater accuracy as well as a saving of time. The author index to a classified bibliography can have its accuracy assured by the taking of a carbon copy of the main entry. Superfluous detail can afterwards be deleted before the slip goes to the printer, or, as is sometimes done, the carbon paper can be cut to omit all but the first two or three lines of the entry. The making of subject index entries at this stage will also be easier and safer as the item will be before one.

3

ARRANGEMENT

'A good bibliography can be read as well as consulted'—
Fredson Bowers.

METHODS OF ARRANGEMENT

The arrangement of entries in a bibliography is of the greatest importance, and the way in which it is done makes all the difference between a mere unwieldy list of titles and a useful and easily consulted reference tool. Both enumerative and descriptive bibliographies need care in arrangement but quite naturally in the latter the stress is on the detailed description of each item and excessive consideration of subject matter will tend to confuse and to detract from the main function. In enumerative bibliography on the other hand, it can be safely said that it is by its arrangement that it stands or falls.

Methods will vary according to the subject and the length of the bibliography, and while it is obviously impossible to consider here every conceivable type of bibliography, we shall attempt to cover the more likely categories. The following methods of arrangement are to be found today:

1 Classified.
2 Subject classed (alphabetico-classed).
3 Alphabetical subject and entry-word.
4 Annalistic.
5 Alphabetical author and/or-title.
6 Dictionary.
7 Place of origin.

We will discuss these in turn and in comparison.

1 Classified

To the experienced bibliographer and librarian, arrangement according to some recognised scheme of classification will recommend itself as the logical and at the same time most detailed method both for general and subject use. It is also one which will appeal to scientists. Further, its successful adoption by the British National Bibliography has long since demonstrated its suitability to national use. It is not likely however to appeal generally to the more conservative student of the humanities who will still prefer alphabetical and/or annalistic arrangement (see below), and is scarcely likely to suit the works of a single author.

In classified arrangement, as in a classified library catalogue, each entry is classified according to an adequate classification scheme, and is assigned a number which in the notation of the scheme is the shorthand abbreviation for the subject of the entry. This will stand at the top left or right of the entry and will govern its position in relation to the other entries. For examples see plates 9 and 10. The obvious advantage of this method of arrangement is that not only items of like subject will be found adjacent to each other, but, if the classification is a rational one, items on related subjects will also be found close at hand.

The commonest classification scheme in library use is the Dewey Decimal Classification. This was at first used by the BNB in its ordinary form but now with considerable emendation to save space (see plate 10). It has been much extended for special bibliographical application—particularly in the sciences—under the name of the Universal Decimal Classification. For an introduction to the UDC see chapter 3 of S C Bradford's *Documentation*, J Mills's *A modern outline of library classification*, chapter 8 and of course the general introduction to the abridged edition. UDC is constantly revised and kept up to date by the Fédération Internationale de Documentation and the English edition has been accepted as a British standard. The abridged version will be found adequate for many purposes. Other schemes, such as the Library of Congress, Brown's Subject Classification or Bliss's Bibliographic Classification, may be used, but none of these is likely to find international adoption as has the UDC in spite of its logical imperfections. Bliss is highly esteemed by many, and has received an increasing amount of attention in libraries of recent years, but the writer knows of no bibliography for which it has so far been employed. A number of technical bibliographies are classified by the UDC including *Physics abstracts* and some learned periodicals and institutions classify their articles and publications in advance, eg *Proceedings of the Institute of Electronic and Radio Engineers* and the British Standards Institution.

When using classified order, it is advantageous as a convenience to the consulter to supply a brief explanation or 'translation' of the class number as follows:

      621.3—*Electrical engineering*

This practice has been popularised by Messrs Palmer and Wells (*The fundamentals of library classification* page 106) under the term 'featuring', the explanatory phrase being the 'feature'. It must be admitted however that while helpful in general bibliographies—it is likely to become impractical in highly technical usage when the advantage afforded by the class number as an abbreviation of a complicated expression will be lost.

A classified bibliography will necessarily have author and subject indexes, and in general bibliographies a title one as well, in addition to an outline at the beginning of the scheme employed. Scientific and technical subjects rarely require title indexes, as items in those fields are commonly referred to by their author's name only.

2 Subject classed

By far the commonest method of arrangement of bibliographies in book form is what we shall call *subject classed*, in order to differentiate it from the *classified* form just described. This consists in effect of a species of classification without a notation and while it may not differ fundamentally from the classified, in practice there are important differences which will be readily discernible.

The items are grouped according to the compiler's own wish under suitable broad divisions of the subject, each of which may be further subdivided as the number of entries falling in any one division makes it desirable. Being an *ad hoc* arrangement it will not necessarily be exhaustive of the subject. Here is a simple example taken from a catalogue of university theses:

Anthropology
    Physical
    Social
Economics
    Agricultural
    Communications
    Finance
    Labour
    Theory
    Trade and tariffs
Education
    General
    History
    Methods
    Psychology

These headings may be further subdivided if need be, eg Economics—Labour—Trade unions, or Education—History—19th century, and so on, according to the size of the bibliography. Subdivision of the subject is rarely likely to be carried to the lengths that it may be in a classified work however—especially under UDC—though when the field is a very limited one it may actually be as detailed. The same result is indeed achieved in two or three stages as would require a long and involved calssification number. An esample will illustrate this:

East African future: a report to the Fabian Colonial Bureau.

In the Dewey Decimal Classification this will receive the rather lengthy number 325.34209676, which can be analysed thus into successive stages of subdivision:

325	Colonisation
325.3	" arranged by mother country
325.34	European colonisation
325.342	British colonisation

44

325.34209	British colonisation —history and local treatment
325.342096	" " in Africa
325.34209676	" " in East Africa

In a subject classed bibliography of colonisation however it will only need to appear under the following successive subdivisions:

British Commonwealth and Empire
    Africa
        East Africa
or alternatively:
    Africa
        East Africa
            British East Africa

As stated above, the degree of subdivision in the subject classed bibliography will be largely dependent on the number of entries falling under any one heading, it being undesirable to have very uneven groups. In other words a division of a subject having a large number of entries grouped under it will be subject to a greater degree of subdivision than an equally general division under which there are few entries. For a hypothetical example, suppose that for a bibliography such as the above one found fifty items on East Africa and only ten on West Africa, one would naturally subdivide East Africa by its parts: Kenya, Uganda, Tanzania, etc, while West Africa would remain undivided.

If the divisions and subdivisions are arranged alphabetically, as they are in the first example in this section, this method is known as the *alphabetico-classed.* In a general bibliography, or one of wide scope, it will be of great assistance to the user, but more often it is thought better to arrange according to what would seem to be a more logical system, based perhaps upon the natural development of the subject. This is the principle on which the best classification schemes are based. Several examples of this arrangement will be found in the next chapter, but the following example in outline (which is not intended to be an exhaustive classification) will illustrate it:

45

LIBRARY SCIENCE
Theory and principles
   The librarian
   Functions of the library
Bibliography
   Historical
   Analytical
   Systematic
Practice
   Classification
   Cataloguing
   Routines
   Assistance to readers
Buildings
   Planning
   Equipment
Libraries by type
   International
   National
   Public
   University
   Special
   School and children's
   Private

This scheme is naturally open to criticism but it must be admitted at least that the juxtaposition of the divisions is more rational than is the following rearrangement, strictly alphabetical:

Bibliography
   Analytical
   Historical
   Systematic
Buildings
   Equipment
   Planning
Libraries by type
   International
   National
   Private
   Public

46

Libraries by type (continued)
  School and children's
  Special
  University
Practice
  Assistance to readers
  Cataloguing
  Classification
  Routine
Theory and principles
  Functions of the library
  The librarian

Many contemporary bibliographies will be found to combine both logical and alphabetical arrangement, and this is often much the most satsifactory, broad alphabetical division being subdivided geographically or chronologically or vice versa; for example:

Fine art	*History*
Schools, A-Z	Period (chronologically)
Each subdivided by period	General
	(Thereafter alpha-
	betically as follows:)
	Ecclesiastical
	Economic
	Educational
	Potitical and constitu-
	tional etc

Within each subdivision the actual entries will be arranged alphabetically by author or in order of publication (see pages 51-52), and there will be an index (see pages 74-75).

The above is advocated for normal subject bibliographies in cases where established classification schemes are inadequate or of subjects in the humanities, eg history, social sciences. It is most easily consulted in book form when two pages are presented to the eye simultaneously and further pages can be flipped over speedily. Much of its virtue will be lost in card form where the visual area is restricted to one entry at a time. There the classified method or that next described is more satsifactory.

3 *Alphabetical subject*

Straightforward subject arrangement differs from 2 above in that each item is arranged alphabetically according to the specific subject or form heading assigned to it, and not under this as a subdivision of a wider subject. The subjects themselves may be subdivided by aspect when necessary, eg GREAT BRITAIN—Social conditions, or AGRICULTURE—Economic aspects.

Taking the same subjects as those given in the first example for 2, we should find them by this method arranged as follows:

>Agriculture—Economic aspects
>Anthropology, Physical
>Anthropology, Social
>Commerce
>Communciations
>Economics
>Education—History
>Education—Methods
>Educational Psychology
>Finance
>Labour and labouring classes
>Social Anthropology *see* Anthro-
>pology, Social
>Tariffs
>Trade *see* Commerce

To librarians this is nothing new. The headings adopted must be based upon a carefully worked out list (such as that of the Library of Congress) to ensure that the same heading is always used for the same subject, and that the whole structure is held together by cross references to overcome the difficulties arising from synonymous terms (eg Trade *see* Commerce) and the relation of one subject to another (Commerce *see also* Communications), the reference being from the greater to the less. It should be clear that such references are very much less necessary in the case of subject-classed arrangement, in view of the grouping of related subjects. Besterman's *World bibliography of bibliographies* and *The London bibliography of the social sciences* (which includes an alphabetico-classed summary of headings to assist users to find the correct heading they want) are examples of this arrangement on a large scale. The writer however favours it for short bibliographies only (up to 300 items), when the subject cannot be suitably subdivided. An author index is essential unless subjects are merged with author and title entries to form a bibliography in 'dictionary' form (see 6 below).

3A *Entry-word*

A variation of this method, and one now somewhat outmoded, is what is known as 'entry-word' arrangement (see Schneider *op cit* page 234). This is a cross between subject and title entry and in it the compiler's choice of headings is in effect limited to the words in the title of the work and the chief task is to decide which of them is most significant.

Under this system

A history of the medieval Church

will probably receive an entry such as:

Church, medieval, history of

It is not recommended for current use in bibliographies but may be employed in indexes.

Before going on to the remaining methods of arrangement, let us compare the relative value of these three most generally applicable ones. With regard to 1 and 3, the late Dr S C Bradford did this with considerable force in his book *Documentation* 2nd edition (pages 56-61). His argument in favour of classified arrangement, which will be supported by most scientists, may be summarised as follows. Arrangement by subject headings is unsatisfactory because a) the subject heading assigned to an item may be ambiguous and items of little or no relationship filed under it; b) it may also be uncertain which of several synonymous terms has been selected for a heading, eg Antennae or Aerials, and numerous 'see' references are needed; c) often the heading has to be a compound expression consisting of several words, eg Electrical apparatus and appliances, Domestic, in which case the chance of synonyms and alternative entry-words becomes greater still, and the possible combinations of words even more considerable; d) apart from this the scattering of related topics and the juxtaposition of unrelated ones means a great deal more labour in tracking down everything written on a subject and necessitates a large number of cross-references linking related subjects such as: Commerce *see also* Finance; Finance *see also* Credit, and so on ad infinitum. Bradford describes this as 'hidden classification', withheld from the public but under the eye of the bibliographer.

Finally there is the question of co-operation. Alphabetical arrangement hampers co-operation with other bibliographies in related fields, even if in the same language, as the terminology employed may differ. In the international sphere the difficulty is aggravated even further in view of the differences in language. The notation of a classification scheme however need have none of these drawbacks.

With most of the foregoing one must agree, though Dr Bradford was not so ready to admit the errors to which the unskilled classifier is liable, and also the differences of opinion that so frequently arise over placings in the best of classification schemes. Classified order is not quite the unambiguous answer to our problem that he suggests. Nevertheless, we must agree that given a well worked out classification scheme—preferably one which receives universal acceptance—and a well trained classifier, it is bound to be more satisfactory than alphabetical subject arrangement for *scientific subjects* and maybe for other *special bibliographies of considerable length*. As has been said, for normal bibliographies the subject-classed method is to be preferred, though where the field is very limited specific subject arrangement (see 3) may be the only one possible. It would be as well to recall Schneider's warning that 'classification schemes cannot last for ever'. New discoveries and approaches to a subject will be bound to necessitate the revision of a classification scheme in the course of time. Fortunately the FID markes full provision for this in its control of the UDC.

Subject classed arrangement lacks many of the drawbacks of specific subject arrangement and possesses some of the advantages of the classified form. Since subjects are grouped under broad heads with subdivisions, ambiguity and synonymous terms will be less likely to occur. An outline of arrangement will be feasible in the preliminaries of the

50

publication, enabling the user to cast his eye over it quickly to discover the class in which his particular interest lies and what heading or headings have been adopted for it.

4 *Annalistic*

Annalistic literally means 'according to year', and, in the bibliographical sense, by year of publication. It is consequently a method of arrangement well suited to those subjects (particularly in the humanities) in which it is important to be able to trace the development as reflected in their literature, eg the works of an author, the editions of a celebrated classic, the history of a movement, the progress of an invention or the products of a printing press. As will be seen from examples given later (pages 63-64), divir on of the field into certain broad catagories may be essential before the annalistic approach is employed, eg the separation of books from periodical contribtuions in the case of an author's works. The method is especially suited to descriptive bibliography.

If it is desirable to distinguish annalistic from chronological arrangement, the latter can be defined as dependent upon the period dealt with by the book or article rather than upon its date of publication. A bibliography of history, for example, may quite naturally be arranged chronologically from the earliest period to the latest. A single historical event however, such as the Battle of Waterloo, might be usefully dealt with annalistically, showing how its documentation has developed through the years from the first despatches to the considered treatises produced in the light of subsequent events and research.

Annalistic sequence of items within a class or subject in a bibliography otherwise arranged will be discussed in due course.

5 *Alphabetical author*

Straightforward alphabetical arrangement by author or title is to be recommended in few cases. Such major bibliographies as use it do so because it is suited to their peculiar intent. For example, Pollard and Redgrave's *Short title catalogue of books printed in England Scotland and Ireland* . . .

51

(*1475-1640*), referred to on page 36, was compiled to record in a convenient format the mere fact of publication and date of works published during the period given, and to assist in the location of copies of them throughout Great Britain by those who already know what authors they are looking for. Likewise Halkett and Laing's invaluable *Dictionary of anonymous and pseudonymous English literature* would be of little use if it were not arranged alphabetically by title, since its function is to identify the author of a book of which one is certain only of the title.

This arrangement is obviously of scant use when we have the more common question to answer: 'What has been written on this subject?', unless used for a small check-list only. The writer knows a large expensive bibliography of literature on former colonial territories running to 670 pages, in which the 16,900 entries are arranged alphabetically by author with a subject index giving references to item numbers only. As can be imagined, there are frequently over a hundred references for larger subjects and the labour involved in following them up among the 16,000 odd entries is exasperating, to say the least. There are nevertheless occasions when a retrospective bibliography of such a general subject as a modern country may be best arranged in this simple way (see page 58).

Of the few cases beyond those already mentioned where this arrangement is important, the trade catalogue is doubtless the most obvious, either under author and title in separate sequences or combined in one. Here the question answered is 'When was this book published?', 'Is it still in print?', or 'What is its price?'. Descriptive bibliographies of pure literature of a particular form and period, annalistic arrangement not being necessary or desirable, are another instance. Michael Sadleir's superb bibliography of *XIX century fiction* (see plate 4) is a case in point. Here annalistic would have been conceivable but might have become unwieldy. The author again is here the most important entry word.

6 *Dictionary*
Dictionary arrangement demands the intercalation alphabetically of entries under author, joint author, title, series

and subject for each item included, *in one sequence.* This is common for library catalogues but not for bibliographies where almost the only examples will be found among the trade lists such as the *Cumulative book index.* The main entry will be under author and those under title and subject somewhat abbreviated. The physical make-up and the demands made upon a bibliography as opposed to a library catalogue render dictionary arrangement unsuitable for the former, where the stress is generally either on the author or on the subject aspect and not on both.

7 *Place of publication or printing*
This method may be regarded as a modification of 2, and is for special use only when the place of origin is the governing factor. This is the case with newspapers and other general periodical literature. Union catalogues of periodicals have in the past been arranged by place of publication even when they were confined to scientific subjects, but this method is not now favoured. Another category of literature to be thus treated is exceptionally rare books such as incunabula. For the latter the so-called 'Proctor order'—countries, towns, presses—has not been superseded. Introduced by Robert Proctor for his *Index to the early printed books in the British Museum,* it is employed by the British Museum *Catalogue of books printed in the XVth century.* It will be discussed in more detail later.

Sequence of titles within a class
After it has been decided what arrangement to adopt for items of differing subject matter, the arrangement of items of like subject matter falling within the same group, class or subject subdivision must be considered. The two possible sequences are a) alphabetical and b) by date of publication. a) is the commonest, most readily comprehended, and with current bibliographies the only possible way. In retrospective work however, arrangement by date may be preferable even in cases other than those already mentioned above under 4 (annalistic) where it is the overall principle. It is bound to be largely a matter of opinion and no hard and fast rule is desirable, although Schneider (*op cit*) says: 'Enter reference works alphabetically and monographs by date.' This however

is a theoretical rather than a practical solution as differentiation is almost impossible and most bibliographies will include both forms of literature. The only recommendation the writer feels constrained to give is that if the subject of the bibliography is such that the date of publication of each item is not of first importance (this applies to many subjects in the humanities though by no means all) alphabetical sequence should be adopted; if the date is vital (as in most scientific works) arrange by date. Whichever sequence is chosen, it must be used throughout. It may be noted that Besterman's *World bibliography of bibliographies* uses annalistic sequence while *A London bibliography of the social sciences* uses alphabetical.

In the examples of application of methods of arrangement to specific subjects which now follow, one or other sequence will be recommended in each case as a guide only.

Computer applications
As already mentioned computer applications in these fields are outlined in chapter 5 together with comment on such suitable indexing systems as PRECIS and KWIC which are preferred by many who regard established classification schemes as inadequate.

APPLICATION TO SPECIFIC SUBJECTS
Having dealt at some length with the more common methods of arrangement, let us now consider their application to special instances. Setting aside national and other general bibliographies, for which the suitability of classified form has already been remarked upon, the sole factor in theory governing the possible compilation of a bibliography of any subject is the existence of literature on that subject. As has been pointed out in chapter 1 however, bibliographies should perform a useful function and satisfy a demand. Here then is a fairly comprehensive selection of the kinds of subjects for which bibliographies are most often wanted with some suggestions for the ways in which they may be treated. It should be clearly understood that these are suggestions only and by no means the sole ways that can be adopted.

1 *A country*

Not a current national bibliography, but the literature on a country wherever published. Except in the cases of very small countries, such as Lesotho or Tristan da Cunha, a retrospective bibliography is almost certain to be selective, as the complete coverage of most countries today must necessarily be effected by separate subject bibliographies. If a reasonably comprehensive list should be attempted for a modern civilised country, running into thousands of entries, classified order should be the obvious choice, for such a work would cover a very large number of subjects—in fact every subject in which there has been literature in relation to the country in question. The treatment of a selective list of 'best books' however (say 200-500 items) should be different. Consideration must be given here to the purpose of the compilation and the public for which it is intended. As likely as not the latter will be people of general outlook in foreign countries, since specialists will know which abstracts etc to consult on their own subjects. Alphabetico-classed arrangement with stress on the social sciences, natural sciences, history, geography and topography, will be best. The peculiarities of each country will naturally be the modifying factor.

Below is a suggested outline for a large civilised country:

General
Art
    General
    Architecture
    Music
    Painting
    Sculpture
    Theatre
Geography
    Cartography
    Economic
    Human
    Physical
    Topography
History
    General
    By broad period

History (continued)
Antiquities
Biography
Language and literature
   (to include introductions to
   the subject and anthologies
   only)
Philology
Drama
Poetry
Prose
Periodical press
Philosophy
Religion
   (subdivide by denominations)
Science, Pure
General
Fauna
Flora
Geology
Science, Applied
Agriculture
Engineering
Medicine
Mining
Other industries
Social sciences
Administration
Commerce
Economic conditions
Education
Law
Politics
Psychology
Social conditions and services.

Sequence of items will be either alphabetical or by date, according to preference—the writer favours the latter.

Note the omission of the mathematical sciences and pure literature. The former are not of sufficient national application in most cases to warrant inclusion and the latter must necessarily be granted a bibliography of its own if it is to be representative. Less developed lands in Africa, the Indies, South America etc must include ethnography. A descriptive bibliography of this nature—witness J A Ferguson's *Bibliography of Australia* (plate 7)—is very suitably arranged annalistically. Such a work is of course of considerable dimensions. In the example quoted, which begins with the year 1784, the fifth; sixth and seventh volumes have reached the year 1900.

A good example of such a bibliography in existence is R L Hill's *Bibliography of the Anglo-Egyptian Sudan from the earliest times to 1937* (OUP, 1939). Here are the divisions chosen by its compiler nearly all of them have been subdivided at length:

Agriculture
Anthropology
Archaeology
Arts
Astronomy
Belles-Lettres
Bibliography
Botany
Chemistry
Communications
Economics
Education
Finance
Forestry
Geography
Geology
Health
History
Hydrography
Irrigation
Language
Law
Meteorology
Periodicals
Religion
Sociology
Zoology

57

This, it will be observed, is in many respects very different grouping from the preceding example, and stands perhaps somewhere between the subject classed and the alphabetical subject arrangement.

An example of an attempt at a comprehensive bibliography of this nature will be found in Oskar Nachod's considerable *Bibliography of the Japanese Empire* 1906-1926 (2 vols., Goldston, 1928).

Finally, although it may seem contradictory, when the accent is on completeness and the intention is a retrospective national bibliography which will be consulted by those—collectors and others—who are not so much concerned with the subject as with the bibliographical detail, a simple alphabetical arrangement is quite acceptable.

2 *A city*

The function of a bibliography of a city varies much from that of the larger unit. Here we have to consider the local historian, the antiquarian and the journalist more than the interested visitor. Most cities have particular associations with persons, events, industries, and the like, and while these must naturally figure in a bibliography they must not be allowed to bulk out of all proportion to the other items—they may well deserve bibliographies of their own. Examples are Lichfield and Dr Samuel Johnson, Sheffield and the cutlery industry or Florence and Renaissance art. Selection is here essential, while in the case of the large centres of printing, such as capitals and old university cities, imprints as such should be completely excluded from a general bibliography.

A bibliography of a European or an American capital city today is a major undertaking and is not being considered in particular here. (See *London bibliography of the social sciences* for a subdivision of LONDON.) The suggested outline below is intended for a city of no especially unusual features:

Administration
(Municipal Services)

Art
  Local artists and musicians
  Collections of pictures
  see also Theatre
Description
  General guide books
  Buildings
  Streets and parks
  Illustrations
  Maps
Education
  Schools
  Technical colleges etc
  Universities
History
  Original sources (records etc)
  By period
  Biography
Industry and trade
  By nature of business
Literature
  Local authors
  The city in literature
Planning
Printing
  Imprints (except in case of
    centres of printing)
Theatres and other entertain-
    ment
  Drama
  Concerts
  Other
Sequence of entries: annalistic

3 *Social sciences*
Possible subjects in this field are very numerous. Alphabetico-
classed or subject-classed arrangement will be satisfactory
with classified if the field is general. The outstanding example of a general bibliography in this field, *A London
bibliography of the social sciences*, is actually arranged

according to the specific subject principle. (*See* 3 Alphabetical subject, *supra*.) A redeeming feature however is the appendix in which the various subject headings are grouped under broader headings such as Agriculture, Economics, Finance, etc, which enables the consulter to discover all the headings employed for related subjects, some of which he might otherwise miss, in the same way that the alphabetico-classed arrangement does. A work of these dimensions however might well have been classified.

We will quote two examples of arrangements that have been used in practice in successful bibliographies in the social sciences:

a) In the field of social anthropology the arrangement used by C R H Taylor in his *Pacific bibliography* (Wellington NZ, 1951) is very sound. The field is first divided into geographical areas eg Polynesia, Melanesia, Micronesia, and then more specifically under smaller groups of islands such as the Solomon and Samoa. In social anthropology geographical area is naturally of the greatest importance. Under each of these headings, wide or narrow, there are the following subdivisions where required with only minor variations:

> Bibliography, general works
> Ethnology, general
> Physical & mental characteristics
> Origins & migration
> Culture contacts
> Tribal & family organisation & law
> Religion & magic
> Science & medicine
> Language
> Folklore
> Music, games etc
> Archaeology, hunting, food, cooking,
>   cannibalism
> Dress, ornament, arts & crafts
> Canoes, artifacts
> Catalogues & museums

This example well illustrates the value of specialised knowledge in a compilation of this kind.

b) Another interesting example is the *International bibliography of sociology*, published by UNESCO, 1952-59, and elsewhere thereafter. Classification is very detailed for the close on 1500 items in each issue, but we can at least give here the ten main divisions:

I   History and organisation of sociological studies
II   Bases, methods and general theories
III   Social structure
IV   Societies, groups and intergroup relations
V   Social control
VI   Social attitudes, public opinion and social communication
VII   Sociology of primitive and insufficiently developed peoples
IX   Social breakdown and disorder *or* Social pathology
X   Applications of sociological knowledge

It may be remarked that in this bibliography all titles not in English or French in the original are given in English in brackets (see plate 8). Subdivision varies much in intensity. As a short example let us quote V (Social control):

Norms, pressures, influences making for conformity
Customs, manners and morals
Conventions, fads, and fashions
Law, sociological aspects
Political institutions and processes
Management, administration, bureaucracy.

While it is possible the compilers may see fit to modify this scheme—terminology has already been changed here and there—any such plan must stand from issue to issue for convenience in consultation. This example should show how inadequate a general classification scheme, such as Dewey, is likely to be for such a subject.

4 *Sciences: pure and applied*
It has already been recommended that scientific subjects should be classified by the Universal Decimal Classification which has been especially evolved for the purpose and is subject to constant revision. In the event of the compiler disagreeing with the classification, which is always possible, he must evolve his own, though this should be done only

after very careful consideration and the comparison of all existing schemes that can be discovered, including those of Bliss and the Library of Congress. For an example of a bibliography arranged by the UDC see plate 9. There must of course be an author index and a key to the classification. The sequence of entries within subdivisions should be annalistic, as the date of publication is of great importance to a scientist.

5 *Pure literature*
The literature of a country or of a language—by no means synonymous—may be covered currently by a national bibliography or a trade catalogue which should include everything traced as published during the week, month, quarter etc, under review. Examples of the former are the *British national bibliography* and *Das schweizer Buch*, and of the latter the *Cumulative book index* and the Dutch *Brinkman*. Compilation of separate current bibliographies confined to pure literature may be thought unnecessary where adequate national or trade bibliographies exist, though they could be useful. Difficult to compile exhaustively, but valuable, would be a current bibliography of English literature published outside the English-speaking world.

Retrospective bibliography of pure literature however is another matter and of particular value to students. If comprehensive as to period, it is almost certain to be selective, listing only works of proved worth. Such a work can in consequence only be undertaken by a scholar or scholars whose authority will be accepted. Examples of these are the *Cambridge bibliography of English literature* and Lanson's *Manuel bibliographique de littérature française moderne*. Division is a) by period and b) by form of literature, though the reverse is conceivable and may be preferred by those who dislike separating periods of literature into watertight compartments.

When the bibliography is limited to a particular form of literature, works by a particular class of writer (eg women, inhabitants of a smaller geographical area), or to special periods, a higher degree of completeness will be expected and is indeed the justification of the work (eg Michael Sadleir's

XIX century fiction). In some young countries, such as Australia, South Africa etc, comprehensive, exhaustive bibliographies are still a possibility—though not always a realisable one for economic reasons—within a comparatively small compass.

6 *Author*

The bibliography of an author may be either descriptive or enumerative. If the subject is an established celebrity in the field of pure literature, or a pioneer of science such as Sir Isaac Newton, whose first editions are sought after, it is likely to be descriptive. In this event arrangement will naturally be annalistic, but should editions subsequent to the first be of sufficient value to warrant inclusion, they should follow the first. It is probable however—and this may apply to other writers beyond those already mentioned—that some such arrangement as the following will be found suitable for the grouping of the different categories of literary product:

1 Collected works (with full analysis of volumes).

2 Separate works (later editions and translations following original. Some bibliographers prefer to relegate translations to a separate section in order to show development of foreign attention to the author's work more clearly). References to contemporary reviews are also useful.

3 Contributions to periodicals.

4 Books, symposia etc, edited and with contributions by author.

5 Selections from works.

6 General studies, obituaries etc.

7 Index of titles and proper names.

Earlier authors may need the category 'Spurious or suppositious works'. Another useful adjunct for writers who publish on both sides of the Atlantic is a table showing comparatively dates and publishers of chief works in the USA and in Great Britain.

The desirability of segregating periodical articles from separate works results from the time lag that usually accompanies the appearance of the latter in comparison with the up to dateness of the former, as well as the difference in physical form. It is important to note however that quite often, especially with poets, an author's work appears first in a periodical. Cross references are highly necessary here from one appearance to another.

As examples of this type of descriptive bibliography one cannot do better than recommend the superb *Soho bibliographies* published by Hart-Davis (see plate 1). For an enumerative example see plate 17.

It should hardly be necessary to emphasise that special circumstances may require a completely different approach. The work of an explorer, for instance, would require careful arrangement under the heads of different expeditions and the inclusion of first despatches as well as later considered accounts in book form.

7 *Single work*
Many of the great books of the world have merited their own bibliographies—eg the *Bible*, Dante's *Divine comedy*, *Pilgrim's progress*, *The Arabian nights* and others which have gone through many editions. In most cases the entries will demand full standard bibliographical description for the sake of satisfactory identification, though a purely enumerative approach will be suitable for less ambitious compilations. The arrangement will naturally be annalistic with year of publication given clearly in the left-hand margin or in the centre of the page. When there are varying impressions within the same year and the order can be definitely determined—from internal evidence or the Term Registers, for instance—well and good, but if the order is not known, difference in place of publication, publisher or printer will be a suitable distinction and the arrangement may be made alphabetically under one of these within any year. Date order however is to be preferred when known.

Unlike an author bibliography where only early editions are commonly included, translations are here best arranged by language separately from the original.

Variations in impressions and editions in rare books may also be conveniently shown in tabular form as an appendix to the bibliography, successive impressions being tabulated horizontally and the variant items vertically. This adjunct may also be used in some author bibliographies. For example:

TABLES FOR THE IDENTIFICATION AND COLLATION OF THE SHAKESPEARE FOLIOS

PRELIMINARY LEAVES

1 Recto blank.
Verso: To the reader.
[Ten lines of verse by Ben Jonson.]
a) Without the engraved portrait.

	I	II	IIIa.
line 2	Shakespeare	Shakespeare	*Shakespeare*
3	Grauer	Graver	*Graver*
5	wit	VVit	*Wit*
7	face;	Face;	*Face;*
8	brasse.	Brasse.	*Brasse.*
signed	B.I.	B.I.	*B.J.*

From *Book handbook* no 2 (1947), the above table is the first of those provided by Mr Reginald Horrox to enable owners of certain leaves from the Shakespeare Folios to identify from which edition they come. The roman numerals I, II and III refer of course to the first, second and third folios, IIIa indicating the earlier or 1663 state of the last-mentioned.

8 *History*

History is an enormous subject and great diversity of opinion will be found as to what should or should not be included under that heading. Some compilers of bibliographies of general history see fit to extend it to cover the political, religious, economic, social and cultural progress of mankind all in the same work. This is done by Frewer in his *Bibliography of historical writings published in Great Britain and the Empire, 1940-45* (Oxford, 1947), who has nineteen classes subdivided by subjects and countries as required. Godfrey Davis in an earlier work: *Bibliography of British history, 1603-1714*, is equally comprehensive in a more specific field. In *A guide to historical literature* edited by G M Dutcher and others (New York, 1949) we have an example of more limited scope and of classified arrangement. It is worth quoting here. There are 26 classes as follows:

A   Historical & Auxiliary Sciences
B   General history
C   Near East in ancient times
D   Ancient Greece
E   Rome
F   Christianity, History of
G   Mohammedanism & Moslem peoples
H   Medieval times, 500-1450
I   Modern Europe, 1450-1870
J   Contemporary times, 1871-1930
K   Exploration & colonial expansion
L   Great Britain & Ireland
M   France
N-Z [Other countries]

Each of these classes may be divided if needed by the following sixteen subdivisions:

1-20	Bibliography
21-40	Encyclopedias etc
41-50	Geography & atlases
51-60	Ethnography
61-100	Source books, collections of sources etc
101-120	Shorter general histories
121-200	Longer general histories
201-500	Histories of special periods, regions
501-530	Diplomatic, military & naval history
531-570	Constitutional & legal history, political theory
571-600	Economic & social history
601-700	Cultural history
701-900	Biography
901-920	Government publications
921-940	Academic & society publications
941-1000	Periodicals

Each of these common subdivisions is denoted by numbers which, used in conjunction with the letter of each division, form the notation of a classification scheme specially adapted to its purpose: for example:

D 571 Economic and social history of Ancient Greece

Q 521 Naval history of Holland

The intermediate numbers are, with the addition of small letters in some cases, used for the actual enumeration of individual works.

History is naturally subject to very considerable specialisation, whether in localities or periods. C L Grose's *A select bibliography of British history, 1660-1760* (Chicago, 1939) is a good example of how a single century may be treated, though the recent *Writings on British history, 1900-1945* compiled for the Royal Historical Society, will probably remain the best example of history bibliography for some time to come. The arrangement in brief is:

I *General*
>Auxiliary sciences
>Bibliography & indexes
>Archives & collections
>Historiography
>British history in general
>English local history & topography
>Wales
>Scotland
>Ireland
>Genealogy
>Collected biography

II *Period history*
>Pre-Conquest
>Medieval period
>Tudor period
>Stuart period
>18th century,
>1714-1815
>1815-1914

Each of the period divisions is subdivided as follows with slight variations:

>General
>Political, constitutional & legal history
>Economic, social & cultural history
>Educational history
>Ecclesiastical history
>Foreign relations
>History of arts & crafts
>Wales
>Scotland
>Ireland
>Biography

The internal arrangement of items is alphabetical throughout. For a specimen page see plate 19.

It will be readily seen from these examples that the classification schemes in regular use would not be as satisfactory for this subject as these are.

8a *Historical personage*
A bibliography of an historical figure is often in demand though good examples are not easy to come by. Those customarily found in biographies are rarely classified. The following, suitably adapted to circumstances, should be adequate for this type of subject:

Biographies, full length.
Incidents in life (in order of event).
Contemporary opinions on and obituaries.
Oratorical works (if any) } May be merged if desirable.
Literary works (if any)
Sub-arrangement of items will in all cases be annalistic.

9 *War*
Schemes of classification for both the first and second world wars have been worked out by the editors of the Dewey Decimal Classification and should prove adequate. Other schemes have of course been drawn up as well. The outline given below, based broadly on Dewey, will give some idea of the classification of the literature of a modern war:

General
Political history
(Outbreak, peace moves etc)
Military history
Naval
Army
Air Force ,
Other (intelligence etc)
Campaigns (arranged chronologically
and geographically)
Other services
Medical
Welfare & educational
Prisoners

Propaganda
Economic aspects
  Food
  Other commodities
  Blockades etc
  (from economic angle)
Civilian life in general
Air raids etc (from civil view-point)
War victims' relief
Civil defence
Humour, fiction, caricature etc

Much further subdivision will of course be needed for a large bibliography, particularly by country. Some may feel it necessary to distinguish between personal reminiscences, of which there are usually an abundance, and formal histories.

10 *Newspapers*

These should be arranged alphabetically under place of publication, not necessarily of printing, as this is not always the same. If however the bibliography is retrospective and also confined to the press of a large city such as London, Paris, or New York, the most logical arrangement would be in order of date of establishment. For a current list intended for general and commercial reference however, this would obviously be only a nuisance. Entry under latest title is to be preferred as that is usually the one best known, but opinions here vary (see pages 27-29). There should be an index of titles. Another very useful adjunct is a chart illustrating by horizontal lines crossing verticals drawn at five-yearly intervals, the birth, run and expiration of any paper. This enables one to see at a glance what was in progress in any year.

A problem which confronts all compilers of newspaper lists is the definition of a newspaper. In the first instance one must admit that it is the format which must weigh heavily in any decision. The best definition one can offer however is that as distinct from a periodical as usually regarded, a newspaper is primarily a chronicle of contemporary events, critical comment being only secondary to its function. A periodical exists primarily to supply commentary or entertainment.

69

There will certainly be doubtful cases which spring to mind, but it is better that they should appear both in a newspaper and a periodical list than be omitted from both.

11 *Periodicals*

Periodicals being of their nature wider in scope than most books, even when of special interest, and also being less numerous, their classification will usually be less intense. In general however the same recommendations will hold good as were put forward for special bibliography of books. As pointed out on page 28, the functions of lists or bibliographies of periodicals may vary—compare Ulrich, Gregory's *Union lists of serials* and the *World list of scientific periodicals*—and will determine the form of entry. These same functions may also determine the arrangement. A trade catalogue such as Ulrich, which is premarily a selection guide, and straightforward bibliographies like the *Index bibliographicus*, should undoubtedly be classified or alphabetically classed. A union catalogue (Gregory, *World list* or *London union list*) intended for the location of sets of periodicals throughout an area, may of course be classified and thus perform a double function, but it is to be presumed that the majority of users will know the titles of the periodicals sought so that alphabetical arrangement is understandable. The economic factor however must enter in when compilations of such size are under consideration. We do not know if Gregory ever entertained the possibility of subject arrangement but clearly the extra work entailed would have increased the cost greatly, and moreover other subject lists are available.

We have still to consider the retrospective list, probably confined to a century or portion of one, and also to a geographical area. There seems no justification here for subject arrangement, and only a slight one for annalistic. Straightforward alphabetical sequence is quite satisfactory, with perhaps a chart showing what periodicals were in progress at any one time.

12 *Imprints—of country, town or press*
(including special catalogues of incunabula)
In most countries the need has been felt for recording systematically the earliest products of the printing press so as to illustrate the development of typography in that country.
a) *Incunabula*: In Europe the study of the earliest printed books has continued for over a century and a half and will occupy scholars for as long again. For historical reasons it cannot be carried out by one country alone and the first great attempt to catalogue European incunabula as a whole was that of Hain in his *Repertorium bibliographicum ad annum* MD (1826-1836), supplemented by later hands. Today we have two still incomplete projects, the *Gesamtkatalog der Wiegendrucke*, A-E, 8 volumes (1925-1978), and the British Museum's (British Library's) *Catalogue of books printed in the XVth century*, 10 volumes (1908-1971), based on such a large collection that it may be regarded as a bibliography. Both Hain and the *Gesamtkatalog* are arranged alphabetically by authors, but it will be admitted that to the student of early printing, authorship is not the most important factor. For that reason the British Library catalogue is arranged by the method introduced by the late Robert Proctor (1868-1903) (Proctor order) in his own valuable catalogue of fifteenth century books on which the British Library catalogue is based. This is first by country, secondly by town, then by press and finally by date of printing, if determinable. The first three take their place according to the date in which printing began in them. Only by arrangement like this has it been found possible to assign books in many cases to their correct printer and date.
There are naturally numerous smaller bibliographies of incunabula seeking to cover individual countries, towns and presses, or merely catalogues of the larger collections such as the Henry E Huntingdon or the John Rylands. In these Proctor order is generally followed. F R Goff's *Incunabula in American libraries; a third census . . .* (New York 1973), arranged by author, is also a fine compilation in this field with an index of printers and publishers.
b) *Early printing other than incunabula:* Forsaking the strict period of incunabula—the fifteenth century—we have

works carrying on into the later centuries such as Sayle's *Early English printed books in the* [Cambridge University] *library 1475-1640.* The latter is arranged by presses, but such catalogues are usually best in purely annalistic order when confined to one country's printing. The British Library's short-title catalogues of books printed in France, Germany, Italy and the Netherlands carry on to the year 1600 with valuable indexes under towns and presses in the last three cases.

Of recent years several of the newer countries of the world outside Europe have been making sure that their 'incunabula' or early imprints, however late in comparison with Europe, shall not be forgotten and the history of printing be the poorer. A good example is Tremaine's *Bibliography of Canadian imprints 1751-1800* and mention has already been made of J A Ferguson's *Bibliography of Australia*. A similar publication has been compiled for the island of Mauritius and its neighbours by its former archivist, A Toussaint. There is still work to be done in this sphere, particularly in descriptive bibliography, and annalistic arrangement of the items is the only possible one.

c) *Presses and publishers.* Compilation in this category may range from incunabula to the products of modern private presses such as the Golden Cockerel. Annalistic is again the obvious method to show development but additional grouping may be found necessary with some of the older presses. A T Hazen's *Bibliography of the Stawberry Hill Press* (Yale UP, 1942), which is an excellent example, is arranged thus:

Books
Appendix A (Odd pieces doubtful)
Bibliography of detached pieces
Appendix B (Doubtful)

'Doubtful' here refers to their attribution to the press.

The famous catalogue of the Ashendene Press is also a model, but not so easy to come by. This includes a specimen page of every product of the Press.

13 *University theses*
A union catalogue of theses and dissertations accepted by a country's universities is a valuable bibliographical tool, the

more so because so many theses are never published and may be overlooked. Such a catalogue should be arranged according to the subjects of the curricula or university departments, as this will be most helpful to students wishing to learn what has already been done in their field of research. There should also be detailed subject and author indexes. It is desirable to note the following information against items when possible:

1 Details of publication, if any.
2 Availability of typescripts on loan or in microform.

Such catalogues will of course be current if possible as is ASLIB's *Index to theses accepted for higher degrees in the universities of Great Britain and Ireland*. Lists of theses presented in special fields are likely now to be more popular. UNESCO's *Theses in the social sciences; an international analytical catalogue of unpublished doctorate theses 1940-1950*, although nearly 30 years old, still presents some interesting features worth noting. Broad subject division was adopted only with further subdivision by language, although all titles were translated into English or French if not in them already. This was sensible in an international bibliography of this kind though by no means obligatory. It is understandable that in enquiring into research in this field the student will be primarily interested in works in his own and other languages with which he is acquainted before going on to unfamiliar ones. The preface to this bibliography is worth study, particularly the section on classification by titles.

SOME OTHER ESSENTIALS

1 *The numbering of items*
In both closed and current bibliographies all items should be numbered, whatever the arrangement. Index references to numbered items are much more satisfactory than to whole pages. In closed bibliographies not in classified form, numeration need not be continuous throughout all sections but can be begun afresh in each one after a capital letter or roman numeral: eg C342 or XV 62. Such numbering will give an immediate indication in the index of the subject or division in which the item has been placed.

Where successive editions are included, these may, in any but a single work bibliography, be assigned lower case letters after the first edition's number; for example:

6 ... 1st edition
6a ... 2nd edition
6b ... 3rd edition

See Donald Gallup's *T S Eliot: a bibliography* for a good example (plate 2). This may also be done with reviews in an author bibliography when they are placed after the works on which they comment.

In current bibliographies the numbering should be continuous throughout each issue, if not a whole year's issues, but it should be prefixed by some code indication of the issue in which it appears, eg 3-2447, which will show at once in the index that the item so designated appears in the third issue of the bibliography in question. In annual publications the last two figures of the year are a better prefix: eg 62-675. In cumulations the natural numerical sequence must of course be upset but items should retain original numbers as an indication of when they first appeared (*cf* BNB).

Even in an intensely classified bibliography where the few entries under any one class number may seem to make separate numeration unnecessary, it should not be dispensed with, if only for the reason just given. Here, as the class number will be above the entry, the item number is better below on the right. In other bibliographies its place may vary but is usually found to the left of the first line of the entry. A variety of placings will be noticed in the examples given throughout this manual.

2 Indexes

Indexes are essential to practically all bibliographies of more than say fifty entries, the only exceptions being those few in dictionary or simple alphabetical author form. (See plate 11).

Author indexes, which include editors, translators, illustrators and the like, should be made always, with references to item numbers. *Title indexes* are required less often and usually only with general, pure literature and author bibliographies. They may be combined with the former.

74

Subject indexes—needed for almost all social bibliographies, bar pure literature and single works—may in the case of classified arrangement refer to class numbers and not to individual items, being in fact an index to the classification. This much reduces the labour in indexing current bibliographies so arranged. In other cases a detailed subject index relative to every item should be made, since the ad hoc arrangement will rarely bring out every facet of the entries' subject content. Each item may have as many index entries as it requires. Here is a simple Example:

Shakespeare's vocabulary in *Love's labour lost*; the effect of the Elizabethan age and the renascence on the creation, use and interpretation of words.

This will doubtless be classed among Shakespeare studies, but in the index it will be referred to from such headings as:

English language, Elizabethan
Love's labour lost, vocabulary
Renascence, effect on language
Semantics
Shakespeare, William, vocabulary

In the case of descriptive bibliography, particularly when concerned with early printing (see 12b above, page 71), an index of printers and/or publishers should be included.

Indexes should be as thorough as possible and synonyms should not be stinted. The actual mechanics of indexing need not be enlarged upon here as there are several good guides to this available (eg R L Collison *Indexes and indexing* Benn, third edition 1969). A suggested method of assisting index making was given on page 40. If this is too elaborate the simple author index to a bibliography in other than alphabetical author order is most naturally prepared by rearranging the cards constituting the basic copy.

3 *Other adjuncts*

Other useful adjuncts to the good bibliography are:
a) Preface, explaining scope, limitations, predecessors etc
b) List of contents, which may include
c) Schedule or outline of the method of arrangement
d) List of authorities consulted and libraries searched etc
e) List of periodicals and other works analysed
f) Elucidation of abbreviations. Here let us again advocate

clear abbreviations—if possible those which are mnemonic and self explanatory to the student who knows his subject; eg BL=British Library, is to be preferred to LB.

g) Explanation in detail of typical entry. If any form other than the standard catalogue entry is used, and particularly in the case of bibliographical description, an example should be taken and analysed part by part. There is no reason why a bibliography should be a cryptic compilation comprehensible only to the expert. Every help should be afforded the inexperienced.

h) In current bibliographies of books, a directory of publishers represented will be very useful. This need not appear however in every issue.

SOME GENERAL CONSIDERATIONS IN ARRANGEMENT

1 *Current bibliographies and cumulations*
Arrangement of current bibliographies should not differ fundamentally from retrospective ones, unless the number of items for inclusion in each issue is so small that alphabetical arrangement by authors is advisable. It should be borne in mind however that new subjects will turn up from time to time and provision must be made for them. With this occasional amendment arrangement must be consistent and not vary from issue to issue; so it is desirable to have an overall plan which will suit both a cumulation of current bibliographies and the individual parts each of which will not necessarily include all the subjects represented in the cumulation. For this reason classified arrangement is really the most satisfactory. Subject-classed arrangement while satisfactory for a cumulation as demonstrated above, may inevitably cause uneven subdivision in the separate parts, but this is not serious compared with inconsistency.

2 *Classifying by title*
The danger of classifying by title when the book or article is not to hand has already been mentioned. There may be times when it cannot be avoided, but it is hardly necessary

to quote examples of misleading titles from which it would be impossible to deduce a book's subject matter, including instances of erroneous location in bibliographies. Do not practice it if the classification is at all intensive. Compare *To the Finland station*, by Edmund Wilson, a history of communism up to the time of Lenin's return to Russia by way of the Finland Station, Petrograd, in 1917.

3 *Repetition of entries*

With the exception of bibliographies in dictionary form (see page 51), where all possible entries are arranged in one alphabetical sequence, entries in a bibliography are not repeated under different headings nearly as much as they are in a library catalogue. In the majority of bibliographies, and certainly in all descriptive bibliographies, each entry will appear once only. In many cases of course there is justification for the inclusion of the same item under more than one heading, such being the comprehensive character of much documentary material, but for reasons of economy and in view of the physical advantages which the book form has over the card file, when it comes to consultation, one main entry for each item is advocated with shortened additional entries giving 'see' references to the main entry. These additional entries will take their normal place in the arrangement, whatever it may be, after this fashion:

Huxley, J S *and* Haddon, A C We Europeans . . . *See no* 42

42 being the number of the full entry for this item. It sometimes happens that there is an authoritative encyclopedic work which deserves mention under many heads in a subject bibliography (compare Hailey's *African survey*). In this event full entries can excusably be made whenever necessary giving the pagination of the relevant parts of the book.

An alternative method to the foregoing and one which saves much more space, is the making of simple 'see also' references to item numbers at the end of each subdivision of the bibliography as follows:

See also: Nos 26, 32, 47, 75

These references may be combined with references to related subdivisions (see pages 48-50).

4 *General bibliography compared with special bibliography*
It should not surprise one to find that there may frequently be considerable differences between the form and content of a) a bibliography of a special subject, and b) the section dealing with the same subject in a work of larger scope. This is due to the need in the former for self-sufficiency which demands the inclusion of borderline cases and of works actually on other subjects which in more general bibliographies would be classed elsewhere with references. The imprecise nature of books and the consequent difference between bibliographical and philosophical classification is partly responsible for this.

A simple example is to be found in the field of geography. Supposing the subject is the travel literature of South Africa, the following comparison will show the different types of books to be expected in the two categories:

a) *Bibliography confined to South Africa*
Travels in SA and its various regions.
Travels in African continent including SA.
General collections of travels including those in SA.
Voyages touching at SA.
Contemporary accounts of flora, fauna and peoples.
Biographies of travellers, missionaries etc.

b) *Section on the subject in a general bibliography*
Travels in SA and its various regions.
Travels in African continent with considerable reference to SA.

A similar position will be found to obtain in many subjects.

4

LAYOUT

IT WAS REMARKED in chapter 1 (pages 16-17) that a bibliography could be presented in various physical forms. Of these the commonest is naturally book form, though services on cards and tapes are popular when up to the minute information is demanded (compare the *Applied science and technology index* in the USA and *De Economische Voorlichtingsdienst* in Holland, and many more). There are of course many instances when bibliographies are produced in response to a personal request, or for the internal use of an institution and one copy only is preserved or maintained.

The fair copy of the work will, as already recommended (pages 31-32), be on cards or slips, and it should not be necessary to spend further time in making a typed copy on paper, unless the reproduction process demands this. If standard catalogue or index cards with the customary hole near the bottom edge are used, a tape can be threaded through these to prevent their sequence being upset at any time.

The essentials of good bibliographical layout are a) clear distinction of one item from another; b) the standing out for easy reference of all headings, both those for sections of the work and those for individual items; and c) the clear distinction of the component parts of the entry, ie author, title, imprint, collation and notes, and of course the class or other number by which it is arranged. These may be satisfactorily produced by the effective use of spacing and, in printing, varied forms of letter, as is illustrated by the examples at the end of this book.

On a typewriter with standard keyboard, the only varieties of letter that can be produced are upper and lower case (commonly called capitals and small letters) and underlining to represent italics, although electric machines are on the market with a larger variety of letters, but their cost is high. It is therefore essential to space items as widely as possible— double spacing as a minimum between each—to lessen the chances of confusion, particularly when it is intended to reduce copy by the offset process (compare plate 14).

Much has been said in chapter 2 on form of entry, but from the layout point of view, standard cataloguing form is the clearest for enumerative bibliography. This gives the author heading, which in bibliographies of authors is naturally not needed for every entry, a line to itself, indents the first line of the title and requires double spacing between collation and notes. In bibliographical usage it is best for the whole annotation to be indented. The first word of the author heading should be in capitals:

HUNT, *Sir* John
The ascent of Everest. London: Hodder & Stoughton, 1953.
xx, 300p. plates, illus. maps. 23cm.
The official account of the successful British expedition, 1953.

More economical of space and only slightly less clear is the following:

HUNT, *Sir* John. The ascent of Everest. London: Hodder & Stoughton. 1953. xx, 300p. plates, illus. maps. 23cm.

Headings for sections and subdivisions should be given at least double the usual space allowed between items (compare *Canadiana*, plate 12). Such headings may be centred but when there are class numbers, these are best on the extreme left or right. In alphabetical subject arrangement headings should be on the extreme left.

Double column is not recommended except where the original typescript is photográphically reduced considerably as even élite type is too large for this to be clear or look well on a normal page.

In descriptive bibliography spacing is even more important to ensure distinction between the different paragraphs of the description (compare the example on pages 23-24 and plates 1, 4 and 6).

In conclusion let us recapitulate some essentials:

1 Let every bibliography be one that will be of practical value;

2 Let the arrangement be one that will be most useful to the public for which it is intended;

3 Be accurate and do not rely upon the work of earlier bibliographers;

4 Beware of false economy of space at the expense of clarity.

5

THE APPLICATION OF COMPUTERS
TO SYSTEMATIC BIBLIOGRAPHY
by N M Lodder

Introduction

Computers have the ability to perform the tasks for which they are programmed consistently, accurately and at very high speed. These abilities are used to greatest advantage when a set of tasks has to be performed over and over again on a large number of items or records. In the compilation of a bibliography several repetitious tasks have to be carried out and the computer can therefore be used to advantage to perform these tasks. This can lead to a saving in time and labour and an improvement in accuracy when compared to manual processes. Not only can computers replace manual procedures but they can provide new and flexible methods whereby records containing bibliographic information can be manipulated and selected.

This flexibility is illustrated by the computer's ability to produce a variety of products from a single record. If the record is suitably coded it can generate author, subject and other index records from it. The computer can also format the bibliographic and index records into the layout required for a particular kind of bibliography and then reproduce them in a variety of forms. It can, for example, produce bibliographies in typeset form, in the form of microfiche catalogues, or of printed cards.

These abilities of the computer can be of assistance to systematic bibliography in two ways:
  i)   in the procedures involved in the compilation of a bibliography, and
  ii) by providing flexible and rapid methods for identifying and retrieving bibliographic information for inclusion in a projected bibliography.

COMPUTERS AND THE PROCEDURES INVOLVED IN COMPILING A BIBLIOGRAPHY

Historical development

The 1960's saw the rapid development of computerised procedures for use in compiling bibliographies. Computer-controlled typesetting techniques and equipment had by then reached an advanced stage of development. These could be used more effectively than manual procedures because of their speed and accuracy. Their introduction into the process of bibliography compilation had become essential because of the large volume of published literature which had to be dealt with and of the rapid increase in the amount of literature published annually. As a result of this a) insufficient human labour was available to process these large volumes manually, b) conventional manual printing procedures were too slow and inflexible to provide suitable bibliographic services to those needing up to date information on the published literature, and c) large special bibliographies, such as Chemical Abstracts, had become cumbersome and difficult to use in their printed form so that new methods of making bibliographic information available had to be found. These difficulties were most evident in the scientific and technical literature.

In 1961 the US National Library of Medicine started development of its Medical Literature Analysis and Retrieval System (MEDLARS). This computerised system was designed to provide i) for the production of Index Medicus and other recurring bibliographies, ii) for the production of smaller special bibliographies when these were needed and iii) for high-speed printing of the bibliographies. A computer-controlled phototypesetter known as Graphic Arts Composing Equipment (GRACE) was designed to provide for the wide range of characters needed for the computer printing of these bibliographies. This, coupled with automatic page formatting, word hyphenation, and line justification capabilities, provided a powerful means of printing. MEDLARS became operational in January 1964.

Similarly the Chemical Abstracts Service of the American Chemical Society started in the 1960's to develop computerised systems for producing its various publications.

The computer was used here not only to assist in the publication process but also in the management of the activities involved in compilation of a large bibliography. For example it was used to keep a record of all published abstracts and to produce a list of periodicals covering chemistry and related fields. The 1960's also saw the first implementations of computers in the compilation of national bibliographies. The Deutsche Bibliographie was the first to be produced in this way (1966). The British National Bibliography and several other national bibliographies soon followed suit.

Standardisation

The development of these computerised procedures generally took place independently in each of the organisations involved in the compilation of bibliographies. As a result the systems which were developed each used different methods. In addition each used a different structure and format in the records in which the bibliographic information was stored. These are the computer-readable records which must be created in any computerised system to enable the computer to process the bibliographic information. Such records are commonly stored on magnetic tape or magnetic disc, but other storage media such as paper tape and punch cards may also be used.

This lack of standardisation was avoided to some extent in the systems developed to produce national bibliographies because it was realised in the early stages of their development that the computer-readable records created by these systems could be of use to all national agencies and to individual libraries. They could, for example, be exchanged between national libraries, so making available to them records for material published in countries other than their own. They could also be used by individual libraries in their own computerised library and information systems.

The US Library of Congress took the initiative in developing a standard record format which would make such an exchange of computer-readable records feasible. This format is known as the Machine Readable Catalogue (MARC) format. It was used experimentally in several computerised

85

library systems during 1966 and 1967. From the experience gained during this experimental period the format was revised, resulting in the so-called MARC II format. This is the format which is still being used as the national US format, although further alterations are still made from time to time.

Other countries followed the US example and developed their own national MARC formats: the UK MARC format used for the British National Bibliography, the Canadian MARC format for Canadiana, the Maschinelles Austausch-format für Bibliotheken (MAB) for use in West Germany, and several others. Although all of these formats were based on the US format they all differed from each other in some respects. These differences resulted from differences in the cataloguing codes used in different countries, in classification codes and subject descriptions used, and from language differences.

This proliferation of national formats led to efforts to develop a more generally accepted format. Amongst these was a group of French-speaking countries (Belgium, France, Switzerland) which worked towards the development of an international MARC format, known as INTERMARC. This group was later joined by other countries, not necessarily French-speaking. The development of an international format was also undertaken by the International Federation of Library Associations and Institutions (IFLA). The work of IFLA culminated in 1977 in its publication of the Universal MARC (UNIMARC) format. This is in the future to become the format used for the international exchange of computer-readable bibliographic records. UNIMARC and the other MARC formats all conform to an international standard for the structure of bibliographic records on magnetic tape. This standard (ISO 2709) was finalised in 1973 by the International Organisation for Standardisation.

Although UNIMARC is to become the international standard, the national formats will continue to be used in their respective countries. This is because differences in cataloguing, classification and subject codes, as well as in language, will still exist. In addition, extensive use of national formats in computerised systems is already being made in countries such as the US and the UK. In these countries it would be impractical to alter the national formats now used to the UNIMARC format. For the purposes of international exchange, however, records in national formats will have to be converted to the UNIMARC format.

The MARC formats provide for the coding of data elements contained in a bibliographic record, for example the title, subject heading, author name and classification numbers. This coding is needed to enable the computer to identify the various elements within a record and so to process them correctly. Three types of code are used:

1 a three-digit code (or tag) used to identify the type of data contained within a section (or field) of a record. In the UNIMARC format tag 200 identifies the field containing title and author information as it appears on the title page of a publication, tag 215 identifies elements describing the physical form (pagination, size, etc) of the publication, and tag 210 elements describing publisher and distributor;

2 two or more indicators which provide supplementary information on the data contained in a field. In UNIMARC the indicators associated with the personal author fields (tags 700, 701 and 702 describe the way in which the author's name is entered ie whether the name is entered under forename, under a single surname, or under a compound surname.

3 Subfield codes which break down the data contained in a field into more specific components. The field for tag 210 (publisher and distributor) includes the subfields coded $a which contains information on the place of publication or distribution, $b the address of the publisher or distributor, $c the name of the publisher or distributor, etc.

Some examples of a UNIMARC-coded record (ᵇ represents a blank):

1 200	1ᵇ$aComputerized library systems$ean introduc-
	tion for library science students$fby James J.
	Johnston ⧸

Explanation: 200 is the tag number used for data relating to the title and author information as it appears on the title page.

87

lb are the two indicators. The first of these, (1) indicates that the title is significant (and should therefore be included for example in a title index). The second indicator is not used in this field and is therefore blank.

The $a subfield contains the title proper, $e contains other title information, and $f the names of those personal or corporate authors responsible for producing the publication as given on the title page.

2 210 | bb$aWashington, D.C.$cThe New Press Co. Inc.

$d1978 ⤸

Explanation: 210 is the tag used for data relating to the publisher, distributor and printer of the publication.

The indicators are not used and both are therefore blank.

$a is the subfield code used to identify the place of publication, distribution etc, $c the name of the publisher, distributor, etc, and $d the date of publication, distribution,etc.

3 700 | b1$aJohnston$bJames J. ⤸

Explanation: 700 is the tag used for data relating to the name of the person who was primarily responsible for the publication.

The two indicators are a blank and a 1 where the digit 1 indicates that the person's name is a single surname.

The $a subfield contains the single surname and the $b the additional parts of the person's name.

Should the computer be required to produce an author index to all records coded in this way, it could be instructed (programmed) to locate the data tagged 700 and its subfields coded $a and $b and to use these data to form the required index entries. In order to sort these index entries into the required sequence it may be necessary for the computer to be able to distinguish between single surnames and multiple surnames (such as hyphenated names). It can do this by checking the second indicator code to see if it is a 1 (single surname), a 2 (multiple surname) or a 0 (the name is a forename and not a surname) and file the names according to the procedures required for these different types of name.

The record fields described above form what is known as the variable field section of a MARC record. This is the section of the record in which the number of fields required and the length of the fields (number of characters contained in a field) will vary from record to record. MARC records contain three other sections:

1 a leader (also known as the Record Label), which appears at the beginning of a record and contains data needed for the purposes of computer processing eg the total length of the record.

2 a Directory, which contains a series of entries giving the tag, length and location of each data field within a record. This therefore forms an index to the variable fields in the record.

3 Control fields, which are fixed length fields containing data which describes certain aspects of a publication eg the language and the date of the publication. These data facilitate the retrieval or selection of records according to criteria such as type of publication (thesis, government publication, bibliography, etc) and date of publication.

The MARC format makes provision for very detailed bibliographic descriptions. Such descriptions are required in a national bibliography which supplies full and authoritative bibliographic information. This detail would not be needed in all bibliographies, in which case an abbreviated form of the MARC format can be used by omitting those fields or subfields not required. It is advisable, however, to use a format which is compatible with the MARC format whenever possible as this will result in uniformity in record structure and coding and make it possible for the computer-readable records created to be exchanged and merged with those of other organisations.

COMPUTERS AND THE IDENTIFICATION AND RETRIEVAL OF BIBLIOGRAPHIC ITEMS

When using computers to assist in compiling a bibliography, the bibliographic information contained in the bibliography is recorded in computer-readable form. Both a printed and a computer-readable version of the bibliography is therefore produced. The computer-readable version was produced initially only because it was needed in the computerised typesetting procedures used to produce a printed bibliography. It was soon realised, however, that the computer-readable records could be used to provide computerised information retrieval services.

Their first large-scale use was as a basis for Selective Dissemination of Information (SDI) services. The purpose of these services is to supply individual users (scientists, technologists, research workers) with regular computer-printed listings of references to recently published literature which deals with topics of specific interest to them. They can be used equally well by someone engaged in the compilation of a bibliography to alert him to references to recent literature relevant to the bibliography which he is compiling.

In an SDI service a set of keywords is compiled for each user. These keywords describe the topic in which he is interested. The Boolean relators AND, OR and NOT are then used to link the keywords together to indicate the required relationship between them. For example, possible keywords to describe the subject "Pollution of freshwater systems (sea water systems are not wanted) by industrial wastes" and their relationship to each other could be:

(River OR Canal OR Stream OR Water) AND (Pollution OR Contamination)
NOT (Sea OR Marine OR Ocean)

Such a set of keywords and relators is known as the users' subject profile. These keywords are matched by the computer against the keywords contained in computer-readable bibliographic records. Records which contain the required keywords and in which the relationship between the keywords also conforms to that specified in the subject profile, are printed by the computer and then despatched to the user.

Following their successful use in SDI services, computer-readable bibliographic records came to be used to provide

90

more sophisticated information retrieval services. In these services it is possible to search the records directly by means of computer terminals which are linked to a computer at which the records are available for immediate access and retrieval. Records are generally stored on devices such as magnetic discs as the computer can locate and retrieve records from this type of device within seconds. Terminals such as video display units or typewriter-like terminals are used. From these terminals the user can conduct a dialogue with the computer. He can enter instructions to the computer by means of the keyboard which forms part of the terminal and the computer can reply by displaying or printing messages or records on the terminal. The method of retrieval used is similar to that used in SDI systems ie keywords and relators such as AND, OR, and NOT are used to describe the topic required. The difference is that when the computer receives the description of a topic, it will immediately respond by informing the user how many records relevant to the topic it has retrieved or by displaying the selected records. The user is able to alter and refine his subject description by altering keywords and relators and by introducing additional restrictions as required. He may for example exclude publications not published within the last two years, not in certain specified languages, or not published in specific journals. This method of searching makes it possible for the user to rapidly select those records most relevant to his needs and to obtain a computer listing of these records.

Several large national and international retrieval services of this interactive type are in operation and generally available. Examples are the services offered from the United States by the Lockheed Aircraft Corporation and the Systems Development Corporation. In 1978 these two organisations had a total of some 80 different bibliographic files available for direct searching from remote terminals. These included such major files as Chemical Abstracts Condensates, Engineering Index (COMPENDEX), Science Abstracts (INSPEC), Psychological Abstracts, Biological Abstracts, and the Library of Congress MARC file.

These SDI and interactive retrieval services can be used effectively by bibliographers to identify items which should be considered for inclusion in a bibliography. They reduce the amount of time which has to be spent in personally scanning printed indexes to identify relevant references. They provide comprehensive coverage of the relevant literature, and very often are more up-to-date than printed indexes and bibliographies. They also provide for more flexible retrieval procedures than can be used with printed indexes and bibliographies.

CONSIDERATIONS IN THE USE OF COMPUTERS

The procedures involved in compiling bibliographies by means of the computer are briefly as follows:

1 bibliographic information is recorded in computer-readable form (encoded) and stored in computer-readable form. Encoding can be done on punched cards, paper tape, or directly onto magnetic tape or magnetic disc. These media can also be used for storage of the records;

2 the encoded information is checked and corrected;

3 the encoded information is entered (input) into the computer from the medium in which it is stored;

4 the computer then processes the information and will

– create from it records, for instance index records, or main bibliographic records which contain the bibliographic information in the form in which it is to appear in a printed bibliography;

– sort the records into the required sequence;

– interfile (merge) the sorted records with previously created records if a cumulation is to be produced;

– format the records into pages and prepare them for computer printing, computer output on to microfilm (COM), or computer typesetting, or for direct display on a computer terminal such as a video display unit;

– control the printing, COM, typesetting or display process.

When a bibliographer is assigned the task of compiling a new bibliography, he should consider whether or not to use computerised procedures to help him in his task. A computer may be an essential aid in some cases whereas in others it may not be practically or economically justifiable. Factors

92

which should be taken into account when considering computerisation are the following:

1 *the size of the bibliography*. The larger the bibliography the more likely that the computer will not only be an economic tool, but will be essential because of the speed of processing and time-saving which results from computerisation and which make it possible for production schedules to be maintained. A small bibliography of a few hundred entries cannot, however, justifiably be computerised.

2 *the form of bibliography*. When a current bibliography is being compiled in which continual updating by the addition of records for newly published material is required, the computer can be used to advantage to perform the necessary filing and merging of the new and old records. In a manual system it is necessary to interfile the new and old records by hand and probably also to re-type the whole bibliography every time an updated or cumulated version has to be printed. Using the computer, this becomes unnecessary as the same computer-readable records can be used over and over again to produce the required cumulated bibliography. For the same reason the computer can be used to advantage when the same bibliographic information has to be made available in different forms. An example of this is a national bibliography which may be published in printed book form and in the form of catalogue cards. This can be achieved without any re-typing or re-encoding of the records because the same computer readable records can be processed by the computer to produce the bibliography in any variety of forms. Depending on its instructions, the computer can produce the bibliography in printed book form, in printed card form, in microfiche or microfilm form, or in the form of computer readable records on magnetic tape.

3 *indexing requirements*. Certain indexing methods lend themselves to computerisation and cannot be used satisfactorily in manual procedures. This is because of the length of time and extensive manpower which will be needed to produce the indexes manually. An example is the Preserved Context Indexing System (PRECIS) developed specifically for use in the computer-produced British National Bibliography. In PRECIS the bibliographer assigns subject

descriptions in natural language to each publication. He also adds special codes which are used by the computer to determine what index entries are to be formed from the subject descriptions and in what format they are to be printed. To compile such entries manually, type them in the correct format, and sort them into the required order is a time-consuming and tedious task which can be carried out far more efficiently and economically by a computer than manually.

Another example is the Keyword-in-Context (KWIC) indexing system which was also designed as a computerised system. In KWIC indexing use is made of keywords in document titles to form index entries. Again the formation of the keyword index entries and their interfiling is more time-consuming and less efficient when done manually than when done by computer.

4 *availability of computer equipment*. There would be no point in contemplating using a computerised system if no computer facilities were available to the bibliographer. Most large organisations have computer facilities, however, and even if these were not available in the organisation itself, the facilities of a computer bureau could be used. If it is really necessary to use a computerised system it is therefore very likely that the necessary computer facilities could be found.

5 *availability of suitable computer programmes*. A bibliographer would seldom be in a position to write the computer programmes needed to produce his bibliography. Training and experience are needed before programming can be successfully undertaken. He may be fortunate enough to be able to have the necessary programmes written for him either by programmers in the library or its parent organisation or to have them written by outside contractors. If this is possible then he will be able to ensure that the computerised system developed conforms to his own specifications. However, special programming may be expensive and will take time to complete. An alternative is to make use of programmes already developed. Many suitable programmes are now available which have been developed by individual libraries for their use or which have been developed by computer suppliers.

Examples are programmes available from some computer companies for the compilation of KWIC indexes. Some organisations also offer computer services which are suitable for compiling bibliographies. In these services the computer processing involved in this compilation will be carried out on behalf of the users of the service. Such services are for example offered by the British Library as part of its British Library Automated Information Service (BLAISE). The bibliographer should therefore first find out if suitable programmes or suitable services are not already available which suit his requirements before he contemplates having programmes specially written for him.

CONCLUSION
There can be no doubt that computers will be used to an increasing extent by bibliographers. This is likely to alter the role and activities of the bibliographer, particularly the bibliographer dealing with scientific and technical subject fields. Greater use will be made of computer-readable bibliographic records than of printed bibliographies for identifying required publications. It is even possible that the printed bibliographies will be completely superseded by their computer-readable equivalents. The bibliographer will make increasing use of computerised procedures to help him in compiling a bibliography. These will greatly ease his task by relieving him of the repetitive activities involved in bibliography compilation.

RECOMMENDED BOOKS

BIBLIOGRAPHY

Besterman, Theodore, *The beginnings of systematic bibliography*. Oxford University Press, second edition 1936.

Bowers, Fredson T, *Principles of bibliographical description*. Princeton University Press, 1949.

Bradford, S C *Documentation*. With an introduction by Dr Jesse H Shera and Margaret E Egan. London, Crosby Lockwood, second edition 1953.

Buhler, C R, McManaway, J G and Wroth, L G *Standards of bibliographical description*. Philadelphia, University of Pennsylvania Press, 1949.

Cowley, J D *Bibliographical description and cataloguing*. London, Grafton, 1939.

Davinson, Donald E *Bibliographical control*. London: Clive Bingley; Hamden, Conn.: Linnet books, 1975.

Esdaile, A J K *A student's manual of bibliography;* revised by R Stokes. London, Allen & Unwin and the Library Association, third edition 1963.

Ferguson, John *Some aspects of bibliography*. Edinburgh, Johnston, 1900.

Gaskell, Philip *A new introduction to bibliography*. Oxford University Press, 1972. Supersedes McKerrow below.

Higgins, M V *Bibliography; a beginner's guide to the making, evaluation and use of bibliographies*. New York, Wilson, 1941.

Larsen, Knud *National bibliographical services; their creation and operation*. Paris, UNESCO, 1953. (UNESCO bibliographical handbooks 1).

Liebaers, Herman 'Shared cataloguing; Part 1. The national programme for acquisitions and cataloguing in the USA;

Part II. The national programme for acquisitions and cataloguing (NPAC) outside the USA'. (In *Unesco bulletin for libraries, V24, 1970, p62-72; 126-154.*)

Loosjes, Th P *On documentation of scientific literature.* (Revised ed.). London: Butterworths, 1973.

McKerrow, R B *An introduction to bibliography for literary students.* Oxford University Press, 1928 (reprinted 1967).

Malclès, L N *Les sources du travail bibliographique.* Genève, Dros, 1950-58. 3 vols in 4. 1 *Bibliographies générales;* 2 *Bibliographies spécialisées (sciences exactes et techniques).* Metuchen: Scarecrow, 1973. Bibliography Translated by J C Hines.

Padwick, E W *Bibliographical method.* London: Jas. Clarke, 1969.

Schneider, Georg *Handbuch der Bibliographie; 4 gänzlich veranderte und stark verm. Aufl.* Leipzig: Hiersemann, 1930.

Schneider, Georg *Theory and history of bibliography*; translated by R R Shaw. New York, Columbia University Press, 1934. (Columbia University studies in library literature series no 1.) *Translation of a theoretical-historical portion of third German edition 1926.*

Shera, Jesse H *Documentation and the organisation of knowledge.* London: Crosby Lockwood, 1966).

CATALOGUING

Anglo-American cataloguing rules. British text. London, the Library Association, 1967.

Anglo-American cataloguing rules. North American text. Chicago, American Library Association, 1967. Second ed. London and Chicago: 1978.

Mann, Margaret *Introduction to cataloguing and the classification of books.* Chicago, American Library Association, second edition 1943.

Sharp, H A *Cataloguing; a textbook for use in libraries.* London, Grafton, Fourth edition 1948.

Tait, James A *Descriptive cataloguing, a student's guide to the 1967 Anglo-American cataloguing rules.* London, Bingley, 1968.

Taylor, M S *Fundamentals of practical cataloguing.* London, Allen & Unwin, 1948.

CLASSIFICATION

Bliss, H E *A bibliographic classification.* New York, Wilson, four volumes 1940-1953.

British Standards Institution *Universal decimal classification.* London, BSI, complete English edition, fourth international edition 1943- (BS 1000). Abridged English edition, London, BS, 1961. (BS 1000A: 1961).

Dewey, Melvil *Decimal classification.* Lake Placid Club New York, Forest Press, seventeenth revised edition 1965.

Foskett, A C *The universal decimal classification; the history, present status and future prospects of a large general classification scheme.* London: Clive Bingley, 1973.

Library of Congress. Decimal classification office. *Guide to the use of Dewey decimal classification, based on the practice of the Decimal classification office of the Library of Congress.* Lake Placid Club New York, Forest Press, 1962.

Merrill, W S *Code for classifiers; principles governing the consistent placing of books in a system of classification.* Chicago, American Library Association, second edition 1939.

Mills, J A modern outline of library classification. London: Chapman & Hall, 1960. (Reprinted 1973.)

Palmer, B I and Wells, A J *The fundamentals of library classification.* London, Allen & Unwin (Practical library handbooks), second edition 1959.

Perreault, J M *An introduction to UDC.* London, Bingley, 1969. Programmed text.

Phillips, W H *A primer of book classification.* London, AAL, fifth edition 1961.

Sayers, W C Berwick *Introduction to library classification.* London, Grafton, ninth edition revised 1958.

Sayers, W C Berwick *A manual of classification for librarians and bibliographers.* London, Deutsch, fourth edition revised by Arthur Maltby 1967.

Haykin, D J *Subject headings; a practical guide.* Washington DC, Government Printing Office, 1951.

Sears, M E and Monroe, I S *List of subject headings.* Ninth edition by B M Westby, New York, Wilson, 1965.

See also for Universal Decimal Classification.

Bradford, S C *Documentation.* Second edition 1953. Chapter 3.

INDEXING

Collison, R L *Indexes and indexing: a guide to the indexing of books, periodicals, music, gramophone records, films and other material, with a reference section and suggestions for further reading.* London, Benn, revised fourth edition, 1972.

Collison, R L *Indexing books: a manual of basic principles.* London, Benn, 1962.

Walsh, J W T *The indexing of books and periodicals.* London, Arnold, 1930.

LAYOUT

Biggs, J R *The use of type the practice of typography.* London, Blandford Press, 1954.

Simon, Oliver *Introduction to typography* edited by David Bland. London, Faber, new edition 1963.

Tarr, J C *How to plan print.* London, Lockwood, 1938.

United Nations. Dag Hammarskjold library. *Bibliographical style manual.* New York, UN, 1963.

REPRODUCTION METHODS

Penrose annual: a review of the graphic arts. London, Lund Humphries, annually.

COMPUTER APPLICATIONS

International Federation of Library Associations and Institutions. Working Group on Content Designators. *UNIMARC Universal MARC format.* London: IFLA International Office for UBC, 1977. 126p. ISBN 0-903043-11-4.

United States. Library of Congress. MARC Development Office. *Books, a MARC format; specifications for magnetic tapes containing catalog records for books* — (Prepared by Gail L Hitchcock and Lenore S Maruyama); 5th ed. Washington: Library of Congress, 1972. 106p. ISBN 0-8444-0019-X

UK MARC manual; first standard edition. London: Bibliographic Services Division, British Library, c.1975. 117p. ISBN 0-900220-47-3.

United States. Library of Congress. Information Systems Office. *The MARC pilot project.* Final report on a project sponsored by the Council on Library Resources, prepared by Henriette D Avram. Washington: Library of Congress, 1968. 183p.

Jeffreys, A E and Wilson, T D *editors. Seminar on the UK MARC Project Southampton, 28-30 March 1969.* London: Oriel Press, 1970.

International Organisation for Standardisation. *Documentation — Format for Bibliographic Information Interchange on Magnetic Tape.* ISO 2709—1973. 4p.

Mauerhoff, G R Selective dissemination of information. In: *Advances in Librarianship*, vol.4, p.25-62. New York: Academic Press, 1974.

Williams, Martha E Data bases—a history of developments and trends from 1966 through 1975. *Journal of the American Society for Information Science*, vol.28 no.2, March 1977, pp.71-78.

Computer-readable bibliographic data bases; a directory and data sourcebook, compiled and edited by Martha E Williams and Sandra H Rouse. Washington: American Society for Information Science, 1976. ISBN 0-87715-114-8.

LIST OF PLATES
(Measurements are of type area)

plate 1   Wade, Allan *A bibliography of the writings of W B Yeats; 3rd ed. rev. and ed. by Russell K Alspach.* London: Rupert Hart-Davis, 1968. (Soho bibliographies I). 17 x 9.3 cm. This, together with the following two examples, illustrates varying styles in the bibliographies of contemporary writers.

plate 2   Gallup, Donald *T S Eliot: a bibliography. New ed.* London: Faber, (1969). 17 x 10 cm.

plate 3   Stott, R T *A bibliography of the works of W Somerset Maugham.* London: Kaye & Ward, (1973). 17.3 x 9.5 cm.

plate 4   Sadleir, Michael *XIX century fiction: a bibliographical record in two volumes. Volume I.* Constable and California University Press; Cambridge University Press (printers). 1951. 22 x 18.5 cm. Based on the author's private collection. A bibliophilic catalogue.

plate 5   Sadleir, Michael *XIX century fiction: a bibliographical record in two volumes. Volume 2.* 1951. 22 x 17.5 cm. An example of the bibliographical treatment of periodical parts.

plate 6   Blanck, Jacob. *'Bibliography of American literature. Volume I.* Yale University Press, 1955. 20 x 14 cm. (full page). Bibliographical description in a small space.

plate 7   Ferguson, J A *Bibliography of Australia. Volume 7: 1851-1900.* Sydney, Angus & Robertson, 1969. 19.5 x 10.5 cm. Retrospective national bibliography of the highest order.

plate 8   *International bibliography of the social sciences, 1975 . . . Social and cultural anthropology*, v.21. London: Tavistock publ., (1978). 20.5 x 12.2 cm. Note the English translation of other than English and French titles.

plate 9   Coblans, Herbert   *A bibliography of chemical research in South Africa*, 1910-1939. Cape Town: African Bookman, 1947. 20 x 11.5 cm. Note the arrangement by the Universal Decimal Classification.

Plate 10   *British national bibliography, 28 June 1978*. 27.5 x 17.5 cm. Arrangment by modified Dewey Decimal Classification with explanation of class numbers. Entries according to ISBD.

plate 11   *British national bibliography*. Author and title index. June 1978. 26.2 x 17.5 cm.

plate 12   *Canadiana: publications of Canadian interest received by the National Library, December 1977*. 24.5 x 18.7 cm. National bibliography with ISBD.

plate 13   *SANB: South African national bibliography / Suid-Afrikaanse nasionale bibliografie, July / September 1978*. Pretoria: State Library. 22 x 13.6.

plate 14   South African Library, Cape Town. *Short-title catalogue of early printed books in South African libraries 1470-1550*. Cape Town: the Library, 1977. 23 x 18 cm. Reproduction from typewriter script with no variety of typeface.

plate 15   *Catalogue de l'édition française 1976: une liste exhaustive des ouvrages disponibles publiés, en français, de par le monde*. Vol.6. Sujets. Paris: 1976. 26.2 x 20 cm. As compact as is compatible with clarity. Compare BNB, plate 10.

plate 16   *Dania polyglotta literature on Denmark in languages other than Danish and books of Danish interest published abroad; an annual bibliography. New series 8 1976*. Copenhagen: the Royal Library, 1977. 21.5 x 14 cm. Small marginal letters indicate language of item.

104

plate 17 Robinson, A M Lewin *William McDougall: a bibliography*. Duke University Press, 1943. 16.5 x 10 cm. An example of good layout and choice of typeface.

plate 18 Centre de documentation économique et Sociale Africaine, Bruxelles. *Alimentation des populations africaines au Sud du Sahara*. Bruxelles, CEDESA, 1965. (Enquêtes bibliographiques XIII). 18.5 x 11.5 cm. With useful summaries of contents that are almost abstracts.

plate 19 Royal Historical Society. *Writings on British history, 1901-1933. Volume 4. 18th century, part I*. London, Cape, 1967. 18 x 11 cm. Brevity and elegance.

plate 20 Schapera, Isaac (*ed*). *Select bibliography of South African native life and problems*. Oxford 1941. 18.5 x 12.5 cm. Still after 38 years a model of good layout and type design.

59

STORIES OF RED HANRAHAN BY | WILLIAM BUTLER
YEATS | THE DUN EMER PRESS | DUNDRUM MCMIV

$8\frac{2}{8} \times 5\frac{3}{4}$; pp. viii, 64: comprising pp. [i–ii] blank; note of limitation of
edition [in red], verso blank, pp. [iii–iv]; title, verso blank, pp. [v–
vi]; acknowledgement [in red], table of contents and woodcut [by
Robert Gregory] on verso, pp. [vii–viii]; text, pp. [1]–[57]; colophon,
in red, on p. [57]; pp. [58–64] blank.

Issued in blue paper boards with buff linen spine; label, printed in
black, carrying title and author's name, pasted on front cover; label,
printed in black, carrying title only, pasted on spine; blue end-papers
matching binding; all edges untrimmed.

500 copies printed on paper made in Ireland and published by
Elizabeth Corbet Yeats at the Dun Emer Press, Dundrum. Finished
on Lady Day in August 1904. Published on May 16, 1905.

Contents

Red Hanrahan
    First appeared in *The Independent Review*, December 1903.
The Twisting of the Rope
Hanrahan and Cathleen the daughter of Hoolihan
Red Hanrahan's Curse
Hanrahan's Vision
    First appeared, under the title *Red Hanrahan's Vision*, in
    McClure's Magazine, March 1905.
The Death of Hanrahan

Most of these stories are rewritten versions of stories from *The Secret
Rose* (No. 21).

In Quinn's copy Yeats wrote "Red Hanrahan is an imaginary name—
I saw it over a shop, or rather part of it over a shop in a Galway
village—but there were many poets like him in the eighteenth century
in Ireland. I wrote these stories first in literary English but I could not
get any sense of the village life with the words. Now, however, Lady
Gregory has helped me, & I think the stories have the emotion of
folklore. They are but half mine now, & often her beautiful idiom is
the better half. W. B. Yeats, June 1905."

Plate 1

A. BOOKS AND PAMPHLETS

A SONG FOR SIMEON [1928]

a. *First edition:*

A SONG FOR | SIMEON | BY T. S. ELIOT | DRAWING BY E. McKNIGHT KAUFFER [London, Faber & Gwyer Ltd.]

Cover-title, 1 blank leaf, [4] pp., 1 blank leaf, incl. 1 col. illus. 18·4 × 12·1 cm. Blue paper wrappers, printed in black on pages [i] and [iv], folded over blank leaves; sewn.

Published 24 September 1928 at 1s. as "The Ariel Poems, No. 16"; 3500 copies printed. *On page [iv] of wrapper:* . . . Printed at The Curwen Press, Plaistow (Unsold copies were reissued in February 1938, in grey paper envelopes, measuring 12·5 × 18·8 cm., printed in red with, on front: . . . The original first printing of the poem, decorated with a drawing by E. McKnight Kauffer . . .)

b. *Signed edition (1928):*

A SONG FOR | SIMEON | BY T. S. ELIOT | DRAWING BY | E. McKNIGHT KAUFFER | LONDON: FABER & GWYER LTD | 1928

6 leaves, 2 blank leaves, incl. 1 col. plate. 22 × 14·2 cm. Off-white paper boards printed in gold on front cover; end-papers; fore and bottom edges untrimmed.

Published 24 October 1928 at 7s. 6d. as "The Ariel Poems, No. 16"; 500 copies printed. *Colophon (recto of first leaf):* This large-paper edition, printed on English hand-made paper, is limited to five hundred copies This is number [*number written in. Signed:* T. S. Eliot.] *On verso of last leaf:* . . . Printed at The Curwen Press, Plaistow

Note: This poem was not separately published in the United States, but it is included in *Collected Poems 1909–1935* ([1936])—A32b—pp. 127–8.

FOR LANCELOT ANDREWES [1928]

a. *First edition:*

FOR LANCELOT ANDREWES | ESSAYS ON STYLE AND ORDER | BY | T. S. ELIOT | [*quotation in 6 lines*] | LONDON | Faber & Gwyer

1 blank leaf, 3 leaves, ix–xi, 13–143 pp. 19·5 × 13·5 cm. Blue cloth boards with tan paper label on spine printed in black and blue; end-papers; fore and

Plate 2

A37   ASHENDEN: or The British Agent   1928

a. First edition:

ASHENDEN | OR | THE BRITISH AGENT | BY | W. SOMER-
SET MAUGHAM | [*publisher's windmill device in box*] | London |
William Heinemann, Ltd. | 1928

Collation: [viii], 304 pp. [ ]⁴ A–T⁸.

p. [i], half-title; p. [ii], BY W. SOMERSET MAUGHAM [listing 10
non-dramatic and 18 dramatic works]; p. [iii], title; p. [iv],
First published 1928 | PRINTED IN GREAT BRITAIN AT THE WINDMILL
PRESS, | KINGSWOOD, SURREY; p. [v], dedication; p. [vi], blank;
p. [vii], fly-title; p. [viii], blank; pp. 1–304, text.

Binding: Dark blue linen-grain cloth, blocked in black on front
with author's symbol and on back with publisher's windmill
device; gold-lettered on front: Ashenden; and on spine: Ashen-
den | W. S. | Maugham | [*in black*] Heinemann.
Plain end-papers; all edges cut; leaves measure 18.3 × 12.4 cm.
Price: 7s. 6d. 10,000 copies were published on 29 March 1928.

Contents: R—*A Domiciliary Visit*—*Miss King*—*The Hairless
Mexican*—*The Dark Woman*—*The Greek*—*A Trip to Paris*—
Guilia Lazzari—*Gustav*—*The Traitor*—*Behind the Scenes*—*His
Excellency*—*The Flip of a Coin*—*A Chance Acquaintance*—*Love and
Russian Literature*—*Mr. Harrington's Washing.*

A37   ASHENDEN: or The British Agent   1928

b. First American edition:

ASHENDEN: *or* THE BRITISH AGENT | *by* W. SOMERSET
MAUGHAM | DOUBLEDAY, DORAN & COMPANY, INC., |
GARDEN CITY, NEW YORK [*dot*] MCMXXVIII

Collation: vi, 304 [306] pp. [unsigned 1–18⁸ 19⁴ 20⁸].

p. [i], half-title; p. [ii], Books by | W. SOMERSET MAUGHAM [listing
13 non-dramatic and 12 dramatic works]; p. [iii], title; p. [iv],
COPYRIGHT 1927, 1928, BY W. SOMERSET | MAUGHAM. ALL RIGHTS
RESERVED. PRINTED | IN THE UNITED STATES AT THE COUNTRY |
LIFE PRESS, GARDEN CITY, N.Y. | FIRST EDITION; p. [v], dedication to
Gerald Kelly; p. [vi], blank; pp. 1–304, text; pp. [305–306],
blank.

Binding: Blue linen calico cloth, blocked in reddish brown on
front with sketch of a sea-horse and lettered in half-circle ASHEN-
DEN; on spine blocked in reddish brown with 3 ornamental

Plate 3
109

LYALL

LYALL, EDNA (1857–1903)

[1454] AUTOBIOGRAPHY OF A SLANDER (The)
Longman etc. 1887.

Copy I: First Edition. Pale grey-blue wrappers, printed in red and black.

Half-title. pp. (viii)+(120)
Spine defective at tail.

[1454a] Copy II: Illustrated Edition. Sq. 8vo. Longman etc. 1892. Smooth navy-blue cloth, elaborately blocked in light blue, white and gold; black end-papers; all edges gilt. Wood-engraved front. and 19 illustrations after L. Speed, all on text paper. Title printed in red and black.

Half-title. pp. (xii) [including front.]+(148) K₂ blank.

Ink signature: 'H. E. Talbot fr. D. T. Sept. 12/ 1892' on half-title. Fine.

[1455] AUTOBIOGRAPHY OF A TRUTH (The)
Longman etc. 1896.

Copy I. Pale grey wrappers, printed in red and black.

Half-title. pp. (viii)+(116) Text ends p. 112 (H₈). I₁ Author's Note, I₂ adverts. Very fine. Ink-signature: 'Priscilla E. Weight. February 1903' on half-title.

[1455a] Copy II. Smooth apple-green cloth lettered in chocolate; black end-papers. Collation as Copy I. Very fine.

HARDY NORSEMAN (A)
3 vols. Hurst & Blackett 1890. Three-quarter smooth blue cloth, blue-green marbled sides, gold-lettered on spine; grey end-papers.
Half-title in each vol., those in II and III single insets.

Vol. I (viii)+302 First leaf of final sig., U₁, a single inset.

II (vi)+302 First leaf of final sig., U₁, a single inset.

III (vi)+(304) Publishers' cat., 8 pp. undated, at end.

Presentation Copy: 'To dear Cousin Martha with the author's love. 1 Oct. 89' in ink on title of Vol. I.

[1459] HINDERERS (The): a Story of the Present Time
Longman etc. 1902. Green linen, mottled in white; black end-papers.

Blank leaf and half-title precede title. pp. (viii) +(184) N₃ N₄ adverts. Very fine.

[1460] IN SPITE OF ALL: a Novel
Hurst & Blackett 1901. Bright brown sand-grain cloth; very dark chocolate end-papers.

Leaf carrying list of works by same Author on verso, and half-title precede title. pp. (viii) +(392) 25₃ 25₄ adverts.

Rubber stamp: 'Major P. G. Shewell, Cotswold, Cheltenham', on verso of fly-leaf and Bookseller's ticket: 'John J. Banks, Cheltenham', inside front cover. Fine.

[1458]

[1459]

[1460]

DONOVAN: a Novel

3 vols. Hurst & Blackett 1882. Smooth blue-grey cloth, blocked in black and lettered in gold; grey-chocolate end-papers.

Half-title in each vol.

Vol. I (vi)+322 pp. (v) (vi), Dedication, and final leaf, Y_1, single insets.

II (iv)+326 First leaf of final sig., Y_1, a single inset.

III (iv)+338 Final leaf, Z_1, a single inset. Publishers' cat., 16 pp. undated, at end.

Binders' ticket: 'Leighton, Son & Hodge', at end of Vol. I. Very fine.

[1457]

DOREEN: the Story of a Singer

Longman etc. 1894. Sage-green linen-grain cloth; black end-papers.

Blank leaf and half-title precede title. pp. (viii)+496

Presentation Copy: 'Hypatia Bradlaugh Bonner. With the Author's Love' in ink on title. (The recipient was Bradlaugh's daughter.)

Note. This book was printed from American plates.

KNIGHT ERRANT

3 vols. Hurst & Blackett 1887. Scarlet sand-grain cloth; black end-papers.

Half-title in each vol.

Vol. I (viii)+300

II (vi)+300 pp. (v) (vi), Contents, form a single inset.

III (vi)+(300) pp. (v) vi, Contents, form a single inset. Publishers' cat., 8 pp. [paged 6] undated, at end.

Ink signature: 'F. Cashel Hoey, March 1887', on half-title of Vol. I. (This is the novelist Mrs Cashel Hoey.) Covers rather soiled.

[1462]

WE TWO: a Novel

3 vols. Hurst & Blackett 1884. Smooth chocolate-brown cloth, blocked in black and lettered in gold; darkish brick-red end-papers.

Half-title in each vol.

Vol. I (vi)+(314) pp. (v) (vi), Dedication, and final leaf, X_5, single insets.

II (iv)+332

III (iv)+(300) U_6 serves as fly-title to Publishers' cat. and carries adverts. on verso. Publishers' cat., 16 pp. undated, at end.

Very fine.

18. TALES OF THE VILLAGE: Third Series. By Rev. F. E. Paget. Published at 3s. 6d. 1841.
19. THE FOREST OF ARDEN: a Tale illustrative of the English Reformation. By Rev. W. Gresley. Published at 4s. 1841.
20. RUTILIUS, or Stories of the Third Age. By Archdeacon Wilberforce. Published at 4s. 1841.

HARRISON'S NOVELIST'S MAGAZINE and NEW NOVELIST'S MAGAZINE [3745]
1780–1788

23 vols. and 2 vols. 8vo. Harrison & Co., 18 Paternoster Row. Full cont. salmon-coloured morocco gilt; marbled end-papers; sprinkled edges. (*New Novelist's Magazine* in dark green, uniform style, but yellow edges and white end-papers.)

Each volume contains an over-all copper-plate title-page giving series title, volume number, contents, vignette and imprint. A sub-title precedes each separate fiction. Plates engraved on copper after Stothard and others, each imprinted and dated, appear as set out in the schedule which follows.

The work was published in weekly numbers (presumably in wrappers, but of what colour or how printed I do not know) and the various novels (each paginated separately) appeared in the order of their sub-title dates. When the series was complete, it was issued as a Magazine of Fiction in 23 volumes, with over-all titles which, like many of the illustrations, had been previously engraved.

I am inclined to think that this set (which came from the Mount Bellew Library in Ireland) was sent out by the publishers in the existing full morocco. Christopher Bellew was the kind of collector to place such an order; and, more suggestive still, the leaf of marbled paper which faces p. 100 of *Tristram Shandy* in Vol. V is absolutely identical with that used throughout for end-papers.

Vol. I. Over-all title-page dated 1780

ALMORAN AND HAMET (Hawkesworth). pp. (54) Sub-title dated 1786. 2 plates: Nov. 1779, May 1780

JOSEPH ANDREWS. pp. (180) Sub-title dated 1785. 4 plates: Dec 1779, Jan. 1780, Feb., March

AMELIA. pp. (300) Sub-title dated 1780. 7 plates: March 1780 (2), April (5)

Vol. II. Over-all title-page dated 1780

SOLYMAN AND ALMENA (Langhorne). pp. (36) Sub-title dated 1787. 1 plate: May 1780

VICAR OF WAKEFIELD. pp. 90 Sub-title dated 1785. 2 plates: May 1780

RODERICK RANDOM. pp. 262 Sub-title dated 1785. 6 plates: June 1780 (4), July (2)

ZADIG (translated by Ashmore from Voltaire). pp. (42) Sub-title dated 1784. 4 plates: July 1780 (2), Aug. (2)

THE DEVIL UPON TWO STICKS. pp. (146) Sub-title dated 1784. 4 plates: July 1780 (2), Aug. (2)

Vol. III. Over-all title-page dated 1781

TALES OF THE GENII ('Sir Charles Morrell'). pp. (236) Sub-title dated 1785. 6 plates: Aug. 1780 (2), Sept. (4)

TOM JONES. pp. (492) Sub-title dated 1787. 12 plates: Sept. 1780 (1), Oct. (4), Nov. (4), Dec. (3)

Vol. IV. Over-all title-page dated 1783

GIL-BLAS. pp. 402 Sub-title dated 1784. 10 plates: Dec. 1780 (2), Jan. 1781 (4), Feb. (4)

ROBINSON CRUSOE. pp. (292) Sub-title dated 1781. 7 plates: March 1781 (5), April (2)

Vol. V. Over-all title-page dated 1786

TRISTRAM SHANDY. pp. 290 Sub-title dated 1787. 8 plates: April 1781 (2), May (4), June (2)

CHINESE TALES (translated by Stackhouse from the French of Gueulette). pp. (116) Sub-title dated 1781. 3 plates. June 1781

THE SISTERS (Dodd). pp. (170) Sub-title dated 1781. 4 plates: July 1781

Vol. VI. Over-all title-page dated 1782

PEREGRINE PICKLE. pp. 438 Sub-title dated 1781. 11 plates: Aug. 1781 (4), Sept. (5), Oct. (2)

MORAL TALES (translated by Dennis and Lloyd from Marmontel). pp. 234 Sub-title dated 1786. 5 plates: Oct. 1781 (2), Nov. (3)

135

Plate 5

141. Margaret Lyon, or, a Work for All. With Other Tales and Poems . . .
Boston: Crosby, Nichols, & Co. 111, Washington Street. 1854.
Printed from magazine plates.
Contains "The Flower's Lesson," pp. 61-63. Reprinted, with slight revisions, in *Flower Fables,* 1855. Also contains "The Little Seed," pp. 119-124.
CWB H

142. FLOWER FABLES . . .
BOSTON: GEORGE W. BRIGGS & CO. 1855.
⟨i-ii⟩, ⟨1⟩-182. Frontispiece and 5 plates inserted. 6⅞" x 4⅜".
⟨1⟩-11⁸, 12⁴.
A cloth: blue; red; slate-blue. T cloth: brown. Yellow end papers. Flyleaves.
Deposited Dec. 18, 1854. Published Dec. 15, 1854-Jan. 1, 1855, according to NLG Jan. 1, 1855. The dedicatory copy at H has an accompanying letter which is marked with date of receipt: Dec. 20, 1854.
H NYPL Y

143. Echoes of Harper's Ferry . . . ⟨compiled by⟩ James Redpath.
Boston: Thayer and Eldridge, 114 and 116 Washington St. 1860.
"With a Rose, That Bloomed on the Day of John Brown's Martyrdom," p. ⟨98⟩.
Deposited May 14, 1860. Published May 15-June 1, 1860 according to BM June 1, 1860.
AAS H NYPL

144. Reports of the School Committee . . . of Concord, Mass. . . . Saturday, March 16, 1861.
Concord: Printed by Benjamin Tolman. 1861.

Printed wrapper.
"Song," pp. ⟨1⟩-2 (*i.e.,* pp. ⟨69-70⟩). Begins: *March, march, mothers and grandmamas!*
H NYPL

145. HOSPITAL SKETCHES . . .
BOSTON: JAMES REDPATH, PUBLISHER, 221 WASHINGTON STREET. 1863.
⟨1⟩-102, blank leaf. 6⅝" x 4⅜".
⟨1-4¹², 5⁴⟩. Signed: ⟨A-B⟩⁶, C-D⁸, ⟨E⟩⁹, F⁸, G⁷.
Printed green boards. Yellow end papers.
Advertised as *in press* APC Sept. 1, 1863, binding not mentioned. Listed, as in boards, APC Sept. 15, 1863. A second edition advertised as *in press* APC Sept. 15, 1863. A new edition advertised APC Oct. 15, 1863. See below under 1869 for an extended edition.
Two printings noted:
1: As above. Bound in printed green boards. Pp. ⟨103-104⟩ blank. Front matter: title-page, p. ⟨1⟩; copyright notice, p. ⟨2⟩; dedication, p. ⟨3⟩; blank, p. ⟨4⟩; table of contents, p. ⟨5⟩; blank, p. ⟨6⟩; advertisement, p. ⟨7⟩; blank, p. ⟨8⟩. On the back cover is an advertisement for Wendell Phillips's *Speeches* and *Life of Toussaint L'Ouverture* which is described as: (*In Preparation*).
2: Noted in cloth only: purple A; green A; purple P. This occurs either with, or without, the title gold-stamped on the front cover. At pp. ⟨103-104⟩ is an advertisement for the fourth edition of Wendell Phillips's *Speeches.* Front matter: title-page, p. ⟨1⟩; copyright notice, p. ⟨2⟩; dedication, p. ⟨3⟩; blank, p. ⟨4⟩; advertisement, p. ⟨5⟩; blank, p. ⟨6⟩; table of contents, p. ⟨7⟩; blank, p. ⟨8⟩.
Collation: ⟨1-2⁶, 3-5¹², 6⁴⟩.
Note: A reprint was issued in printed wrapper as No. 6 of *Redpath's Books for the Camp Fire Series.* Imprint: *Boston: James Redpath, Publisher, 221 Washington Street. New York: The*

27

Plate 6

114

G PROBLEMS OF KNOWLEDGE, ARTS AND SCIENCE, FOLK TRADITIONS
PROBLEMES DE LA CONNAISSANCE, ARTS ET SCIENCES, TRADITIONS POPULAIRES

G.o GENERAL WORKS
OUVRAGES GÉNÉRAUX

G.o1 Theoretical studies
Études théoriques

5178 BIGSBY, C. W. E. *et al.* "La tradition, la culture populaire et la société", *Cultures* 1(2), 73 : 13–125.

5179 ČISTOV, K. V. "Specifika fol'klora v svete teorii informacii" (The specificity of folklore in the light of information theory), in: *Tipologičeskie Issledovanija po Fol'kloru.* Moskva, 75 : 26–43.

5180 CORTÁZAR, A. R. "Los fenómenos folklóricos y su contexto humano y cultural: concepción funcional y dinámica" (The folklorical phenomenons and their human and cultural context: functional and dynamic conception), *Folkl. amer.* 18, 74 : 15–50, bibliogr.

5181 DÍAZ CASTILLO, R. "En defensa de la tradición popular" (In defense of folk tradition), *Folkl. amer.* 18, 74 : 173–190.

5182 DUNDES, Alan. *Analytic essays in folklore.* Paris–The Hague, Mouton, 75, xii–265 p., bibliogr., index. (Studies in folklore).

5183 DUSSEL, E. "Cultura imperial, cultura ilustrada y liberación de la cultura popular" (Imperial culture and the liberation of folk culture), *Stromata* 39(1–2), 74 : 93–123.

5184 GEERTZ, Clifford (ed.). *Myth, symbol and culture.* New York, W. W. Norton, 74, xi–227 p., index. [Originally published in *Daédalus*, 1972.]

5185 IVANKOV, V. M. "Izvčenie A. N. Afanas'evym folk'klora kak sredstva vyraženija narodnogo mirovozrenija" (The study of folklore by A. N. Afanasev as a means of expression of folk world view), in: *Voprosy Filologii i metodiki issledovanija.* Voronež, 75 : 29–48.

5186 KOLESOV, M. S. "Fol'klor i socialističeskaja kul'tura" (Folklore and socialist culture), in: *Muzyka v socialističeskom Obščestve 2.* Leningrad, 75 : 74–117.

5187 KRAWCZYK, V. "Structural analysis of folklore in the light of most recent research", *Lud* 19(2), 75 : 32–34.

5188 PUTILOV, B. N. "Osnovnye aspekty svjazi fol'klora s tradicionno-bytovoj kul'turoj" (Basic aspects of the relations of folklore with traditional social culture), *Sov. Étnogr.* 2, 75 : 3–11. [English summary.]

5189 PUTILOV, B. N. "Problemy fol'klora v trudah V. Ja. Proppa" (Folklore problems in the works of V. Ja. Propp), in: *Tipologičeskie Issledovanija po fol'kloru.* Moskva, 75 : 7–15.

5190 RUBIN DE LA BORBOLLA, D. F. "Notes sur les métiers d'art", *Cultures* 2(3), 75 : 105–108.

5191 SQUILLACCIOTTI, M. "Cultura egemonica e culture subalterne" (Hegemonical culture and subordinate culture), *Etnol. Antropol. cult.* 2, 75 : 78–85. [By A. M. Cirese; review article.]

258

Plate 7

115

Stratton, Charles S. "General Tom Thumb".

Sketch | of the | Life, Personal Appearance, Character & Manners | of | Charles S. Stratton, | the man in miniature, known as | General Tom Thumb, | and his wife, | Lavinia Warren .Stratton, | the famous | Commodore Nutt, | and the infinitesimal | Minnie Warren, | together with | comic illustrations | of their | travels and adventures. | ——— | Melbourne: | Fergusson and Moore, Printers, 48 Flinders Lane East.

Sq. 12mo. Pp. 44. Pp. 9-44 consist of comic pictures. N.D. [*c.* 1868]. Sewn.

Stratton was born in Bridgeport, Connecticut, U.S.A., on January 4, 1838. At 18 months his growth was arrested and, though his health was good, his stature remained exceedingly diminutive. Trained by Mr. Barnum, he toured the United States and Europe, and appeared before Queen Victoria and other sovereigns and princes. In 1863 he married Miss Lavinia Warren, making a final tour of the world in 1864.

Copies: Mackaness; M.L.; N.L.   16324

Stray Leaves from the Diary of an Indian Officer.

Stray Leaves | from the | Diary of an Indian Officer, | containing an | Account of the Famous Temple of Juggurnath, | its daily ceremonies and annual festivals, | and | a residence in Australia. | === | London: | Whitfield, Green & Son, 178, Strand. | ——— | 1865.

8vo. Pp. xii, 300. Green embossed cloth boards, on front cover: Gateway of the Taj (in gold) and on spine in gold lettering: Stray | Leaves | from the | Diary | of an | Indian Officer, also decorations. Five illustrations.

The author describes himself as a retired officer of Her Majesty's Bengal army. For health reasons he visited Sydney and resided there for a time (see Chapters xxiv and xxv). Later he revisited Sydney and visited Hobart (Chapters xxxi and xxxii).

Copies: F.C.; M.L.; N.L.; P.L. S.A.   16325

Streams of Life.

Streams of Life | Refresh the Weary | and | Impart Vitality to All! | ——— | [Quotation] | ——— | Sydney: | George Loxton & Co., General Printers, | 42 New Pitt Street. | ——— | 1875.

8vo. Pp. viii, 160. Coloured frontispiece: "The Stranger's Grave". Cream wrappers. Title repeated in full on front cover within border of rules. Sewn.

According to the Preface "this publication was designed, with the intention of getting at least Five Thousand Copies circulated throughout the colony during the present year, 1875, in the hope of making it known, in as simple a way as possible, under various phases, the love of God to man, and the way of a sinner's salvation. . . ." Anonymous preface is dated: New South Wales, | 1st March, 1875.

Copies: D.L.; M.L.   16326

The Same. Green wrappers. Sewn. Coloured frontispiece: "The Stranger's Grave" is a different drawing from No. 16326.

Copies: D.L.; M.L.; N.L.   16327

Plate 8
116

541 THEORETICAL CHEMISTRY

541.11 THERMO-CHEMISTRY

541.11   1
SCHWARTZ, E. and COBLANS, H.
Lösungs—und Verdünnungswärmen von
Salzen von der äusserstten Verdünnung
bis zur Sättigung.
Z. phys. Chem.A, 176, 430-43, 1936.
(Thesis based on this work, carried out at
University of Munich, presented by Coblans,
for Ph.D. (S.A.), 1937.)

541.12 CHEMICAL MECHANICS

541.12 : 536.775   2
TROMP, F. J. A new method of applying
the principles involved in the phase rule.
J. chem. metall. Min. Soc. S. Afr., 35, 34-41,
1934-35.

541.12 : 536.775   3
TROMP, F.J. Application of the phase rule
to systems containing distant phases.
J. chem. metall. Min. Soc. S. Afr., 36, 143-5,
1935-36.

541.122.3   4
DENISON, R. B. Chemical combination in
liquid binary mixtures as determined by a
study of property-composition curves.
Trans. Faraday Soc., 8, 35-50, 1912.

541.122.3   5
DENISON, R. B. Formation of chemical
compounds in homogeneous liquid systems.
A contribution to the theory of concen-
trated solutions.
S. Afr. J. Sci., 10, 132-47, 1912.

541.122.3   6
DENISON, R. B. Property-composition
curves and the molecular changes which
take place on forming binary liquid mixtures.
Trans. Faraday Soc., 8, 20-34, 1912.

541.123   7
TROMP, F. J. and de LOOR, B. The
absorption of gases by liquids and solids
with particular reference to hydrogen and
palladium.
J. chem. metall. Min. Soc. S. Afr., 35,
168-81, 1934-35.

541.123.2   8
TAMMANN, G. and KRIGE, G. J. R.
Die Gleichgewichtsdrucke von Gashydrate.
Z. anorg. Chem., 146, 179-95, 1925.
(Experimental work carried out at the
University of Göttingen)

541.123.2.034   9
SMEATH, THOMAS J. and RAMSAY,
A. G. The partial pressures of sulphuric
acid over concentrated aqueous solutions
of the acid at high temperature.
J. chem. Soc., 123, 3256-70, 1923.

541.123.2.034   10
SMEATH, THOMAS J. and BARKER,
W. F. The partial pressures of water vapour
and of sulphuric acid vapour over concentrated solutions of sulphuric acid at high
temperatures.
J. chem. Soc., 127, 2820-31, 1925.

541.123.21
Aqueous solution. See 546.289.4

541.123.31   11
PELLING, A. J. The system chloride—
sulphate—sodium—water.
J. S. Afr. chem. Inst., 8, (1), 3-6, 1925.

541.123.31 : 547.495.2   12
du TOIT, D. F. Evenwichten in stelsels
samengesteld uit ureum, water en een of
meer zuren.
Proefschrift (D. Chem.)—Leiden, 1914.

541.123.5   13
PELLING, A. J. and ROBERTSON, J. B.
The reciprocal salt pair sodium chloride
and calcium nitrate.
S. Afr. J. Sci., 20, 236-40, 1923. 21, 196-205,
1924.

541.123.5   14
ROBERTSON, J. B. The reciprocal salt
pair sodium bichromate and potassium
chloride.
J. Soc. chem. Ind., Lond., 43, 334-8T, 1924.
(Experimental work carried out at the
University of Edinburgh.)

541.127
Reaction velocity. See 542.943 :

1

Plate 9
117

428.6 — ENGLISH LANGUAGE. READING BOOKS
428'.6 — English language. Reading books. *Primary school texts*
Flowerdew, Phyllis
 More interest / [by] Phyllis Flowerdew. — Edinburgh : Oliver
 and Boyd. — (Wide range reading)
 Quiz book 3. — 1978. — 32p : ill ; 21cm.
 ISBN 0-05-003065-5 Sd : £0.40
 1.Ti 2.Sr
(B78-19114)
 Quiz book 4. — 1978. — 32p : ill ; 21cm.
 ISBN 0-05-003066-3 Sd : £0.40
 1.Ti 2.Sr
(B78-19115)

Heaslip, Peter C
 The terraced house books / [by Peter C. Heaslip] : [photographs
 by John Bennett]. — London : Methuen. — (Methuen's resources
 for reading : early reading)
 [Set A]. — 1978. — 4v. : col ill ; 15x21cm.
 ISBN 0-423-50470-3 Sd : £1.75
 1.Ti 2.Bennett, John
(B78-19116)
 [Set B]. — 1978. — 4v. : col ill ; 15x21cm.
 ISBN 0-423-50480-0 Sd : £1.75
 1.Ti 2.Bennett, John
(B78-19117)

Murphy, Frank
 Stepping-stones. — Dublin : Educational Company of Ireland.
 Authors: F. and D.M. Murphy.
 Basic reader B / [illustrations by John Skelton]. — 1978. — 32.[3]p : col
 ill ; 21cm.
 Sd : £0.44
 1.Ti 2.Murphy, Donal M 3.Skelton, John, b.1924
(B78-19118)
 Extension reader B / [illustrations by John Skelton]. — 1978. — 32.[3]p
 col ill ; 21cm.
 Sd : £0.44
 1.Ti 2.Murphy, Donal M 3.Skelton, John, b.1924
(B78-19119)

**428'.6 — English language. Reading books. Special subjects: Great
 Britain. Agricultural industries. Farms.** *For coloured
 immigrants*
Owen, Evan
 Lower End Farm / [by] Evan Owen ; illustrated by Anna
 Dzierzak. — Glasgow [etc.] : Blackie, 1978. — [2],30p : ill ; 22cm.
 — (Owen, Evan. Living in Britain)
 ISBN 0-216-90508-7 Pbk : £0.78
 1.Ti
(B78-19120)

**428'.6 — English language. Reading books. Special subjects: Great
 Britain. Travel.** *For coloured immigrants*
Owen, Evan
 Getting there / [by] Evan Owen ; illustrated by Douglas Phillips.
 — Glasgow [etc.] : Blackie, 1978. — [2],30p : ill ; 22cm. —
 (Owen, Evan. Living in Britain)
 ISBN 0-216-90507-9 Pbk : £0.78
 1.Ti
(B78-19121)

428'.6 — English language. Reading books. Special subjects: History.
 Primary school texts
Snellgrove, Laurence Ernest
 Wide range history / [by] L.E. Snellgrove ; reading consultant
 Phyllis Flowerdew. — Edinburgh : Oliver and Boyd. — (Wide
 range reading)
 1. — 1978. — 128p : ill(some col), col map ; 20cm.
 ISBN 0-05-003052-3 Pbk : £0.90
 1.Ti 2.Sr
(B78-19122)

428'.6'2 — English language. Reading books. *For illiterate adults*
Belina, Tom
 Flight to fear / [by] Tom Belina. — London : J. Murray, 1978. —
 [3],59p : ill ; 18cm. — (A bestellers book)
 Originally published: Belmont, Calif. : Fearon-Pitman, 1977?.
 ISBN 0-7195-3519-0 Pbk : £0.65
 1.Ti
(B78-19123)

Campbell, Archie
 Diamonds in the dirt / [by] Archie Campbell. — London : J.
 Murray, 1978. — [3],44p : ill ; 18cm. — (A bestellers book)
 Originally published: Belmont, Calif. : Fearon-Pitman, 1977?.
 ISBN 0-7195-3523-9 Pbk : £0.65
 1.Ti 2.Sr
(B78-19124)

D'Amelio, Dan
 Silvabamba / [by] Dan D'Amelio. — London : J. Murray, 1978.
 — [3],60p ; 18cm. — (A bestellers book)
 Originally published: Belmont, Calif. : Fearon-Pitman, 1977?.
 ISBN 0-7195-3526-3 Pbk : £0.65
 1.Ti 2.Sr
(B78-19125)

Dorre, Pamela
 Wind over Stonehenge / [by] Pamela Dorre. — London : J.
 Murray, 1978. — [3],59p : ill ; 18cm. — (A bestellers book)
 Originally published: Belmont, Calif. : Fearon-Pitman, 1977?.
 ISBN 0-7195-3512-3 Pbk : £0.65
 1.Ti 2.Sr
(B78-19126)

McAuliffe, Jim
 Three mile house / [by] Jim McAuliffe. — London : J. Murray,
 1978. — [3],60p : ill ; 18cm. — (A bestellers book)
 Originally published: Belmont, Calif. : Fearon-Pitman, 1977?.
 ISBN 0-7195-3516-6 Pbk : £0.65
 1.Ti 2.Sr
(B78-19127)

Salas, Nichole
 Night of the kachina / [by] Nichole Salas. — London : J. Murray,
 1978. — [3],44p : ill ; 18cm. — (A bestellers book)
 Originally published: Belmont, Calif. : Fearon-Pitman, 1977?.
 ISBN 0-7195-3524-7 Pbk : £0.65
 1.Ti 2.Sr
(B78-19128)

428'.6'2 — English language. Reading books. *For slow learning
 adolescents*
Wilson, Robert L
 Spies. — London : Edward Arnold, July 1978. — [48]p. —
 (Headlines ; 8)
 ISBN 0-7131-0251-9 Lp : £0.75 : CIP entry
 1.Ti 2.Sr
(B78-19129)

438 — GERMAN LANGUAGE USAGE
438'.3'421 — Spoken German language. *Exercises, worked examples*
Hammond, Robin T
 Fortbildung in der deutschen Sprache / by Robin T. Hammond.
 — London : Oxford University Press.
 Originally published: 1969.
 Teacher's book. — 1971. — [2],21p ; 24cm.
 Bibl.: p.16-17.
 ISBN 0-19-912004-8 Sd : £0.25
 1.Ti
(B78-19130)

448 — FRENCH LANGUAGE USAGE
448'.3'421 — Spoken French language. Comprehension. *Exercises,
 worked examples. Secondary school texts*
Hunt, C
 Vous avez bien compris?. — London : Hodder and Stoughton,
 July 1978. — [64]p.
 ISBN 0-340-22353-7 Lp : £1.20 : CIP entry
 1.Ti 2.Rice, J M 3.Hunt, B
(B78-19131)

482 — GREEK LANGUAGE. ETYMOLOGY
482'.2 — English language. Comprehension. *Programmed texts*
Harnadek, Anita
 Critical reading improvement : a program for self-instruction /
 [by] Anita Harnadek. — 2nd ed. — New York ; London [etc.] :
 McGraw-Hill, 1978. — [7],182p ; 24cm. — (McGraw-Hill basic
 skills)
 With answers. — Previous ed.: New York : McGraw-Hill, 1969.
 ISBN 0-07-044412-9 Pbk : £4.45
 1.Ti
(B78-19132)

500 — SCIENCE
507'.2'04 — Science. Research. Policies of European Community.
 European Community countries
 Strategies for Europe. — Oxford : Pergamon, July 1978. — [178]p.
 ISBN 0-08-022992-1 : £10.00 : CIP entry
 1.Goldsmith, Maurice 2.Science Policy Foundation 3.European Economic
 Community
(B78-19133)

507'.2041 — Science. Research organisations. Great Britain. *Science
 Research Council (Great Britain). Reports, surveys. Serials*
Science Research Council *(Great Britain)*
 Report of the Council for the year [ended 31st March] ... /
 Science Research Council. — London : H.M.S.O.
 1975-76. — [1976]. — v,100p,[8]p of plates : ill ; 25cm. — ([1975-76 H.C.]
 635)
 ISBN 0-10-263576-5 Sd : £1.75
 1.Ti
(B78-19134)

510 — MATHEMATICS
510 — Mathematics. *Middle school texts*
School Mathematics Project
 SMP 7-13 / the School Mathematics Project. — Cambridge
 [etc.] : Cambridge University Press.
 Unit 3. Assessment tests. — 1978. — [238]p ; 30cm.
 ISBN 0-521-21654-0 Sd : £2.00
 1.Ti
(B78-19135)

Plate 10

118

Plate 11

119

C811'.5'4   PS8523*
Layton, Irving, 1912–
    The covenant / Irving Layton. – Toronto : McClelland and Stewart, c1977.
    112 p. ; 23 cm.
    Poems.
    ISBN 0 7710 4832 7 pa. : $4.95
    I. Title.
    Full name: Layton, Irving Peter
           C77-1333-3

C811'.5'4   PS8576*
Maltman, Kim, 1950–
    The country of the mapmakers / by Kim Maltman. – [Fredericton, N.B.] : Fiddlehead Poetry Books, 1977.
    · 127 p. ; 23 cm.
    Poems.
    ISBN 0 920110 24 X pa. : $14.
    I. Title.
           C77-1353-8

C811'.5'4   PS8575*
McIlwain, Sandy, 1950–
    And between us, the night / by Sandy McIlwain. – Fredericton, N.B. : Fiddlehead Poetry Books, 1977.
    27 p. ; 22 cm.
    ISBN 0 920110 26 6 pa. : $2.50
    I. Title.
    Full name: McIlwain, Donald John Alexander
           C77-1408-9

C811'.5'4   PS8575*
McNeill, Julie, 1957–
    Ching the well : symbol of an unchanging source, drink deep or taste not / [by Julie McNeill]. – Toronto : H.K. Miyamoto, 1976.
    [27] p. ; 14 cm.
    Poems.
    pa. Processed : $1. H.K. Miyamoto, 335 Dundas St. East, Toronto, Ont. M5A 2A2
    I. Title.
    Full name: McNeil, Julie Ann
           C77-12820-3

C811'.5'4   PS8576*
Morgan, John Hanly
    Hands of friends / John Hanly Morgan. – Toronto : J. H. Morgan, c1977.
    96 p. ; 21 cm.
    Poems.
    pa. J. Morgan, Apt. 2815, 40 Homewood Ave., Toronto, Ont. M4Y 2K2
    I. Title.
           C77-13197-2

C811'.5'4   PS8526*
Moyer, Kenneth A., 1913–
    Catch a falling star : a galaxy of church poems / by Kenneth A. Moyer. – [s.l. : s.n., 1976]
    70 p. ; 29 cm.
    Cover title.
    pa. Processed : $2.75 K. A. Moyer, P.O. Box 25, Elmira, Ont. N3B 2Z5
    I. Title.
    Full name: Kenneth Allan Moyer.
           C77-9928-9

C811'.5'4   PS8576*
Mrkich, Dan, 1939–
    The white spectre / Dan Mrkich. – Ottawa : Commoners' Pub., 1977.
    [24] p. ; 22 cm.
    Poems.
    ISBN 0 88970 024 9 pa.
    I. Title.
           C77-13378-9

C811'.5'4   PS8527*
Newlove, John, 1938–
    The fat man : selected poems, 1962–1972 / John Newlove. – Toronto : McClelland and Stewart, c1977.
    127 p. ; 23 cm.
    ISBN 0 7710 6733 X pa. : $4.95
    I. Title.
           C77-1337-6

C811'.5'4   PS8527*
Nichol, B. P., 1944–
    The marlyrology books 1 & 2 / B. P. Nichol. – 2d ed. – Toronto : Coach House Press, 1977.
    [240] p. : ill. ; 23 cm.
    Poems.
    pa. $6
    I. Title.
           C77-12998-6

C811'.5'4   PS8577*
Nichols, F. Eleanor
    Sunshine and shadows : poems / by F. Eleanor Nichols. – [s.l. : s.n.]. c1974
    54 p. ; 23 cm.
    F. Nichols, R.R. # 1, Waterdown, Ont. L0R 2H0
    I. Title.
           C77-12876-9

C811'.5'4   PS8531*
Perry, Wib, 1916–
    Love, fun & other things : a book of verse / by Wib Perry. – [s.l. : s.n.]. c1975 (Vancouver : College Printers)
    x, 60 p. : ill. ; 20 cm.
    pa. $3.95
    I. Title.
    Full name: Wilbert A. Perry.
           C77-10586-6

C811'.5'408   PS8283*
Haiku / Kenton Public School, Grade 5, Room 204, 1975. – [North York, Ont.] : Board of Education for the Borough of North York. [1975]
    34 p. : ill. ; 22 cm.
    Cover title: Haiku at Kenton, 1975
    pa. Processed : 50c. Limited to libraries, teachers and academic institutions. Kenton Public School, 34 Kenton Drive, Willowdale, Ont. M2R 2H8
    1. Haiku, Canadian (English) 2. School verse – Kenton Public School, Willowdale, Ont.
    1. Haiku canadien-anglais 2. Écoliers. Poésie d' – Kenton Public School, Willowdale, Ont.
    I. Kenton Public School, Willowdale, Ont. II. North York Board of Education (Ont.) III. Title: Haiku at Kenton, 1975
           C77-10834-2

C811'.5'408   E98*
La Macaza poems / [poetry contributed by Vance Bear et al ; woodcut prints by Walter Jacobs et al. ; edited by Vivian Hayward]. – La Macaza, Que. : Manitou Community College : Thunderbird Press. [197–]
    43 p. : ill. ; 22 cm.
    pa. Processed : $1.50
    1. Canadian poetry (English) – Indian authors 2. Canadian poetry (English) – La Macaza, Que. 3. College verse – Manitou Community College, La Macaza, Que.
    1. Poésie canadienne-anglaise – Auteurs indiens 2. Poésie canadienne-anglaise – La Macaza, Québec 3. Étudiants, Poésie d' – Manitou Community College, La Macaza, Québec.
    I. Bear, Vance. II. Jacobs, Walter. III. Hayward, Vivian. IV. Manitou Community College, La Macaza, Que.
           C76-7820-3

811'.5'408   PS586
Other Americans / Richard Latta ... [et al.]. – Toronto : [s.n.], 197–?]
    [8] p. ; 28 cm. – (Gronk series 7, 8)
    pa. Processed.
    1. American poetry – 20th century 2. Concrete poetry, American.

Plate 12

120

000
GENERALITIES / ALGEMEENHEDE

001.5532016
Cape of Good Hope (Province) : Library Service
16 [Sixteen]mm films: accessions 1970-1974 —
016.0015532 Cape of Good Hope

001.5532016
Kaap die Goeie Hoop (Provinsie) .
Biblioteekdienste 16 [Sestien]mm films:
aanwinste 1970-74 — 016.0015532 Kaap die Goeie
Hoop

010/019
BIBLIOGRAPHIES AND
DOCUMENTATION / BIBLIOGRAFIEÉ
EN KATALOGUSSE

015.68 - 839.36
Nienaber , Petrus Johannes samest.
Bibliografje van Afrikaanse boeke: dl. 8, 1
Januarie 1971-31 Desember 1974/ [saamgestel
deur] P.J. Nienaber. - Johannesburg: Perskor,
1977. - 360p.; 22cm.
ISBN 0 628 01017 6: R16,50.

(77/1787)

016.0015532 - 001.5532016
Cape of Good Hope (Province) . Library
Service
16 [Sixteen]mm films: accessions 1970-1974/
Cape Provincial Library Service. - Cape Town: The
Library. [1975]. - 222p.; 31cm.
Gratis.

016.0015532 - 001.5532016
Kaap die Goeie Hoop (Provinsie) .
Biblioteekdienste
16 [Sestien]mm films: aanwinste 1970-74/ Kaap-
se Provinsiale Biblioteekdiens. - Kaapstad: Die
Biblioteek. [1975]. - 222p.; 31cm.
Gratis.

016.3900968 - 390.0968016
Van Warmelo , Nicolaas Jacobus comp.
Anthropology of Southern Africa in periodicals
to 1950: an analysis and index/ compiled under
direction of N.J. van Warmelo. - Johannesburg:
Witwatersrand University Press, 1977. - 1484p.:
map; 31cm.
ISBN 0 85494 378 1: R60,00.

(77/1585)

016.5568 - 556.8016
South Africa (Republic) . Geological
Survey
Bibliography and subject index of South African
geology 1974/ Geological Survey. - Pretoria: Go-
vernment Printer, [1976]. - 113p.; 30cm.
ISBN 0 621 03503 3: R2,20(South Africa).
R2.75(overseas). Post free.

016.82 - 820.16
University of South Africa . Library.
Subject Reference Department
A Pilot bibliography of South African English
literature from the beginnings to 1971/ compiled
by Subject Reference Department, Library, Univer-
sity of South Africa; edited by D.R. Beeton. -
Pretoria: University of South Africa, 1976. -
xii, 104p.; 21cm. - (University of South Africa.
Documenta; No. 14).
ISBN 0 86981 072 3: R4,75.

(77/1580)

016.92657 - 926.57016
Cunningham , Anna McCubbin comp.
Howard Pim papers/ compiled by Anna M. Cunning-
ham. - Johannesburg: Library, University of the
Witwatersrand, 1976. - vi, 52p.; 30cm. - (Univer-
sity of the Witwatersrand. Library. Historical
and literary papers. Inventories of collections;
No. 03).
ISBN 0 85494 376 5: R2,50.

(A77/0458)

020
LIBRARY SCIENCE /
BIBLIOTEEKKUNDE

025.171
South Africa (Republic) . Parliament.
Senate
Senate Amendments to Archives Amendment Bill.
[B3 and 3A-77](Assembly). - [Pretoria: Govern-
ment Printer], 1977. - [2]p.; 30cm. - (South
Africa (Republic). B. series: 1977; No.
03B/1977).
Teks in Afrikaans en Engels.
ISBN 0 621 03146 1: 5c(South Africa). 10c(over-
seas). Post free.

025.171
Suid-Afrika (Republiek) . Parlement.
Senaat
Senaat-amendemente op Wysigingswetsontwerp op
Argiewe. [W. 3 en 3A-77](Volksraad). - Preto-
ria: Staatsdrukker], 1977. - [2]p.; 30cm. -
(Suid-Afrika (Republiek). W.-reeks: 1977; No.
003B/1977).
Text in English and Afrikaans.
ISBN 0 621 03146 1: 5c(Suid-Afrika). 10c(oor-
see). Posvry.

026.968
Musiker , Reuben
The Africana collections of the University of
the Witwatersrand by Reuben Musiker. - Johannesburg: University of the Witwatersrand, 1976. -
21p.: ill.; 21cm. - (University of the Witwatersrand. Library. Occasional publications; No. 01).
Bibliography:p.21.
ISBN 0 85494 419 2: R1,50.

(77 1793)

1

Plate 13
121

337. MARIANUS de Genazano
Cora] Innocentio Pont. Maximo oratio habita Dominica
tercia adventus. Rome: Stephan Planck, 19 Dec.
1487. 4to.
BM: IA18459   PEPL

338. MARTIALIS, Marcus Valerius
Epigrammata. Venice: Vindelinus de Spira. [n.a.
1473]. 4to.
BM: IB19581; Goff: M-297   SAL(G)

339. ----- ---- Venice: Johannes de Colonia &, Johannes
Manthen, 1475. Fo.
Border decoration by Charles Bell, mid-19th
century.
BM: IB20242; Goff: M-300   SAL(G)

340. MARTIANUS MINEUS FELIX CAPELLA
De nuptis philologiae et Mercurii libri duo.
Vicenza: Henricus de Sancto Ursio, 16 Dec. 1499.
Fo.
BM: 167.e.13; Goff: C-117   H. Adler

MARULLUS, Michael
see TARCHANIOTA MARULLUS, Michael

341. MARY, the Blessed Virgin
Privilegia sanctissimae virginis Mariae. Vienna:
Johann Winterburg, [c. 1500]. 4to.
BM: IA51557; Goff: P-975; Oates: 4025
UW

347. MELA, Pomponius
De orbis situ libri tres. Paris: Christian Wechel,
1540. Fo.
Includes Oronce Finé's map: Nova et integra
universa orbis descriptio, 1531, inserted.
BM: 570.g.23   JPL

348. MELANCHTHON, Philipp
Annotationes ... Verzaichnung unnd kurczliche
anzayggung des rechten und aygentlichen verstands
der Epistel die S. Paulus zū den Rhomern geschribē
hat verdeūtscht. Augsburg: [possibly Simprecht
Ruff], 1523. 4to.
                                               SAL(G)

349. MENSA PHILOSOPHICA
Mensa philosophica. Louvain: Johannes de
Paderborn (Westphalia), [c. 1485]. 4to.
Attributed variously to Theobaldus Anguilbertus
Hybernensis, and to Michael Scotus. (BMC).
Quire 1 supplied in ms.
BM: IA49270; Goff: M-494   SAL(G)

350. MERLIN
Senluyt le premier volume de Merlin; le second
volume de Merlin; les prophecies de Merlin.
Paris: A lenseigne de la rose blanche couronnee
[P. le Noir], 2 jun. 1526.
3v. printed together, each with separate
colophon.
cf. BM: 683.f.24-26
                                               SAL(G)

MICHAEL SCOTUS
see SCOTT, Sir Michael

MARY, the Blessed Virgin
    see also ALBERTUS MAGNUS. Opus insigne de
    laudibus beate Marie.

342. MARZIO, Galeotto
    De doctrina promiscua liber. Florence: Lorenzo
    Torrentino, 1548. 8vo.
        BM: 73.b.4
                        UND

343. MASSARIUS, Franciscus
    In nonum Plinii De naturali historia librum castiga-
    tiones & annotationes.   Basel: Hieronymus
    Frobenius & Nicolaus Episcopius, 1537.   4to.
        BM: 924.f.26
                        PEPL

344. MAUROCENUS, Paulus
    [De generatione aeterna et temporali Christi]. Opus
    de aeterna temporalique Christi generatione. Padua:
    Bartholomaeus Campanus Ponticuruanus, 28 Apr. 1473.
    8vo.
        Also attributed to the printers Bartholomaeus de
    Valdezoccho and Martinus de Septem Arboribus.
        BM: IA29816; Goff: M-380; Oates: 2538
                        SAL(G)

123

345. MELA, Pomponius
    Cosmographia; sive, De situ orbis. [Venice:
    "Printer of Pomponius Mela", c. 1477]. 4to.
        BM has variant (IA24843) dated "Venice,
    15 Nov. 1477."
        BM: IA24844; Goff: M-448
                        SAL(G)

346. ---- De orbis situ libri tres. Basel: Andread Cratander,
    1522. Fo.
        BM: C.32.m.5(1)
                  UP   *Plate 14*

MODESTUS
    De re militari
        see SCRIPTORES rei militaris

MONTALBODDO, Antonio Fracanzano da
        see FRACAN, Montalboddo

351. MORE, Sir Thomas, St.
    The Cofutacyon of Tyndales answere made by syr
    Thomas More, knyght lorde chaūcellour of Englonde.
    London: William Rastell, 1532. Fo.
        Reply to William Tyndale's "Answere vnto Sir
    Thomas Mores dialoge."
        BM: G.12078; STC: 18079
                        SAL(G)

352. ---- A dyalogue of syr Thomas More knyghte ...
    wherin be treated dyvers maters, as of the venera-
    tion & worshyp of ymagys & relygnes, prayng to
    sayntys, & goyng ō pylgrymage ... (London:
    Johannes Rastell, 1529). Fo.
        BM: C.37.h.10; STC: 18084
                        SAL(G)

353. MÜNSTER, Sebastian
    Cosmographia. Beschreibung aller Lender.
    Basel: Heinrich Petri, 1544. Fo.
        BM: Maps. 45.d.31
                        JPL

354. ---- Horologiographia, post priorem aeditionem per
    Sebast. Munsterum recognita [2 ed.] Basel:
    Heinrich Petri, 1533. 4to.
        BM: 532.d.21
                        UND

796.35 Tennis

Apprendre le tennis. ESTRABEAU, - FEUILLET. - 1952, 192 p., 14x20 [Table Ronde] 225-280-7B 6,35

En place pour un set DAIGNAULT, Pierre - 1964, 116 p., ill., [Homme] 044-663-3B C$ 1,00

La Fabuleuse histoire du tennis. QUIDET, Christian - 1976, ill., [O.D.I.L.] 446-478-0A 125,00

Lawn-tennis. [Bornemann] (Sportive) 048-250-5B 4,50

Mon tennis. LAVER, Rod - - Traduit de l'Anglais. 1971, 316 p., 13x20 [Solar] (Sports 2001) 237-163-1B 25,70

Nadase superstar. DELAMARRE, Gilles - 1974, 218 p., [Solar] (Sports 2004) 376-049-3B 23,30

Précis de tennis moderne. PELLETIER, René P. - [Bornemann] (Sportive) 048-265-3B 12,00

Santé et joie de vivre par la raquette. JOLICOEUR, Roger - 1974, 63 p. ill., [Lidec] 432-904-1B C$ 1,90

Techniques du tennis. ELLWANGER, Rico - - Traduit de l'Allemand. 1975, 164 p. ill., [Homme] 411-387-4B C$ 4,00

Le tennis 1974, 96 p. ill., 12x20 [B M] 370-149-7B 9,90

Le tennis. 11,5x11,5 [Gérard] (Flash No.99) 224-862-3B 6,00

Tennis. Bibliographie. 24 p. [Québec Off.] 400-897-5B C$,40

Tennis. Technique, jeu, entrainement, pédagogie. CHOQUET, Jack - 1976, 360 p., ill., 16x24 [Amphora] 427-358-7B 48,00

Le tennis COCHET, Henri - 1965, 3 ed., [Colin] 089-246-3B 7,00

Le tennis. COCHET, Henri - 3 ed., 11,5x17,6 [P.U.F.] (Q.S.J. No.084) 050-509-9B 6,90

Le Tennis. DEFLASSIEUX, Alain - 1976, 92 p., ill., 20,5x20,7 [Chancerel] 435-089-8A 23,00

Le tennis. Techniques et progression. DEFLASSIEUX, Alain - 92 p., ill., 20,5x20,7 [Chancerel] (Vidi) 445-198-5A 23,00

Le tennis. La technique, la tactique, l'entrainement. DENIAU, Georges - 1974, 152 p., ill., 15,5x24 [Laffont] 362-574-6B 34,00

Le tennis. L'apprendre, le jouer, l'enseigner. FAULKNER, Edwin J. - WEYMULLER, Frédérick - - Traduit de l'Anglais. 1974, 294 p., ill., 24x26 [Gérard] 377-103-7B 44,00

Le tennis. L'apprendre, le jouer, l'enseigner. FAULKNER, Edwin J.- WEYMULLER. Frederick. - 1975, 256 p., ill., 16x23,5 [Gérard] 406-838-3B 44,00

Le tennis LALANNE, Denis - [Table Ronde] (Domaine du Sport) 071-050-9B 7,50

Le tennis. LORIN, Philippe - COUVERCELLE, Jean - 1976, 48 p., ill., 21x24,5 [Denoel] (Connaissance et technique) 434-233-3A 28,00

Le tennis. PETRA, Yvon - [Bornemann] (Sportive) 048-264-6B 8,00

Le tennis. TALBERT, Bill - - Traduit de l'Anglais. 1974, 94 p., ill., [B M] 414-948-0B 9,90

Le Golf. 100 nouvelles lecons. PLAYER, Gary - 92 p., ill., 20,5x20,7 [Chancerel] (Vidi) 445-200-9A 23,00

Le Golf. 100 nouvelles lecons. PLAYER, Guy - 1976, 92 p., ill., 20,5x20,7 [Chancerel] 435-093-0A 23,00

Le golf. PRICE, Charles - 1974, 93 p., ill., [B M] 414-952-2B 9,90

Golf au Québec. Guide du golfeur 1969. 1969, 144 p., [Excellence, Ed.] 166-292-3B C$ 2,00

Golf. La technique, la tactique, l'entrainement. GARIALDE, Jean - LAFAURIE, André-Jean - 1976, 208 p., 15,5x24 [Laffont] 414-457-8B 49,00

Golf, 55 scores. NICKLAUS, Jack - [S.F.L.] (Mes loisirs) 234-342-1B ,40

Le golf-miniature. LAURENT, Claude-Marcel - - Dans le même ouvrage: Règle du jeu,installation d'un terrain! 32 p., ill., 13,5x18,5 [Bornemann] (Jeux et règles) 155-207-4B 4,50

Pour un golf puissant et précis. PLAYER, G. - 128 p., ill., 17x25,5 [S.F.L.] (Mes loisirs) 234-943-9B 42,00

Techniques du golf. BRIEN, Luc - 1973, 172 p., ill., [Homme] 367-392-8B C$ 3,50

796.4 Gymnastique. Athlétisme

L'athlétisme. 1974, 96 p., ill., 12x20 [B M] 370-146-3B 9,90

Athlétisme féminin. KENNEDY, Robert - PARKER, Virginia - - Traduit de l'Américain. 1972, 115 p., 13,8x22 [Vigot] 356-911-8B 24,00

L'athlétisme. GARDIEN, André - HOUVION, Maurice - PROST, Raymond Thomas - 1972, 128 p., 11,5x17,6 [P.U.F.] (Q.S.J. No.1476) 279-039-2B 6,90

L'athlétisme. MEYER, Gaston - [Table Ronde] (Domaine du Sport) 071-103-6B 10,00

L'athlétisme. - 1. La course vitesse, haies, demi-fond, fond. O'DUNAWAY, James - 1974, 96 p., ill., [B M] 414-950-6B 9,90

L'athlétisme. - 1. Demi-fond, fond cross, steeple. VIVES, J.- [Bornemann] (Sportive) 048-255-4B 6,00

L'athlétisme. - 2. Vitesse, relais, haies. VIVES, J.- [Bornemann] (Sportive) 048-256-2B 6,00

L'athlétisme. - 3. Hauteur, longueur, triple saut perche. VIVES, J.- [Bornemann] (Sportive) 205-037-5B 6,00

L'athlétisme. - 4. Poids, disque, javelot, marteau. VIVES, J.- [Bornemann] (Sportive) 048-257-0B 6,00

Athlétisme et natation. La pratique des sports individuels. BATTISTA, Eric - PORTES, Maurice - 1973, 146 p., ill., 11,5x15,5 [Fleurus] (Série 100 No.51) 317-922-3A 10,00

Le parcours sportif du sapeur-pompier. Reglement officiel, étude comparative et commentaires pratiques. ALLEMANDOU, Pierre - 2 ed., [France-Sélection] 403-826-1B 7,00

Perche. Bibliographie. 24 p., [Québec Off.] 400-908-0B C$,40

Poids. Bibliographie. 24 p., [Québec Off.] 400-951-5B C$,40

Stages internationaux 'Fond Romeu 1971'. [Francaise, Féd. ed. phy. gym.] 403-770-1B 20,00

Toujours en pleine forme. VAN WEYENBERGH, Claire - 1975, 253 p., 16x22 [Gérard] 426-556-7A 32,00

Triple saut. Bibliographie. 24 p., [Québec Off.] 400-907-2B C$,40

Vive la Canadienne Jocelyne Bourassa. BARRETTE, Jacques - 1973, 95 p., ill., 20x13,5 [Homme] 377-164-9B 19,50

Yoga et diététique. [Lasserre] 440-982-7B 39,60

796.41 Exercices de souplesse et de force. Yoga

ABC de l'éducation physique féminine. CHAMPETIER DE RIBES, Ebba - [Chiron] 084-557-8B 4,90

L'ABC du Hatha-Yoga. FAVRE, Norette - 1958, 80 p., [France, Cercle Livre] 069-017-2B C$ 1,50

Aperçus sur le Kriya-yoga. Voie d'évolution rapide. ATRI, Rishi - 1972, 112 p. ill., 19x15 [Auna Bodha Satsanga] 408-675-7B 21,00

Les Arts martiaux en trois jours. MORVAN DENEGRE, Frank - 1976, 224 p., ill., 10,4x21 [Solar] 435-055-9B 28,00

Atlas d'Education physique. WILLEMS, Y. - [De Boeck] 149-001-0B FB 325,00

Les bases psychologiques de l'éducation physique. LOISEL, Ernest - 1974, 6 ed., 13,5x21,5 [Colin] (Traités éducation physique) 089-249-7B 27,80

Le bonheur par la conscience de soi, yoga de l'Occident. SURYAKANTA, - 1975, 144 p., 11x18 [Epi] 406-342-6B 25,00

Chassez la fatigue, en retrouvant la forme. Culture physique et détente pour tous les ages. ROUET, Marcel - 1975, 261 p., ill., 16x24 [Dangles] 443-025-2B 42,00

La Confédération suisse et l'éducation physique de la jeunesse. BURGENER, Louis - La Chaux-de-Fonds, 1952 - Bibliographie, Fac. sim., [Kraus] 255-263-6A nü 123,00

Connaissance et technique du HathaYoga. RUCHPAUL, Eva - [Denoel] 043-547-9A 38,00

Corps et âme en harmonie. DELZA, Sophie - ill., 14x21 [Denoel] 044-218-6B 11,00

Cours de culture physique ou Hatha-yoga par correspondance. VILLETTE, A. - 1962, 21x27 [Villette, A.] 360-863-5B 3,00

Le tennis de A à Z. COCHET, Henri – FEUILLET, Jacques – 1970, 296 p., ill., 14x20 [Table Ronde] *(Ordre du Jour)*
247-361-9B C$ 2,50

Le tennis de table. Règles officielles de a F.F.T.T. [Bornemann] *(Sportive)*
225-256-7B 22,00
048-251-3B 4,50

Le tennis de table. 11,5x11,5 [Gérard] *(Fla;A No.84)*
6,00

Tennis de table. AGOPOFF, Alex – 4 ed., ill., [Amphora] *(Sports)*
224-854-0B
208-790-6B 21,00

Le Tennis de table. SECRETIN, Jacques – 1976, 64 p., ill., 12x18 [Solar] *(Solorama)*
443-291-0B 12,00

Tennis de Table pour tous. COURTIER, Jean-Paul – LAFARGUE, Jean Claude – 1974, 96 p., ill., 13,5x18,5 [Bornemann] *(Sportive)*
374-885-2B 13,00

Tennis en trois jours. LOTH, Jean-Paul – 1975, 220 p., ill., 10x21 [Solar] *(En trois jours)*
414-156-0B 25,00

Le tennis en 10 leçons. Et tout pour jouer de A à Z. DARMON, Pierre COUVERCELLE, Jean – 1973, 216 p., 14x20 [Hachette] *(En 10 leçons)*
316-789-7B 27,60

Le tennis en 13 leçons. GARDINI, Fauste – – Traduit de l'italien. 1973, 190 p., 14,5x21 [Vecchi, ed.]
312-756-0A 19,50

Tennis facile avec Yvon Petra. PETRA, Yvon – 1976, 96 p., ill., 15,5x24 [Bornemann]
434-802-5B 23,00

Tennis total. DENIAU, Georges – 1970, 08 p., ill., 10,5x21 [Jeune Parque]
245-130-0B 21,60

Tennis 74-75, le bilan d'une année. 1975, 224 p., ill., 21x28 [Laffont]
406-120-6B 84,00

796.36 Golf

Le baseball. 1969. [Homme]
044-759-9B C$ 2,50

Baseball-Montréal. LEBLANC, Bertrand B. – 192 p., ill., [Jour]
146-674-7B C$ 3,00

Le code du golf, sur les parcours et les règles de Saint-Andrews. GOLIAS, Roger – SIMONNET, André – 1973, 176 p., 13,5x21 *(Chiron)*
318-948-7B 30,00

Comment se sortir du trou au golf. BRIEN, Luc – 1975, 199 p., ill., [Homme]
411-383-3B C$ 4,00

Connaissance et technique de golf. DAMPIERRE, Gérard de – 1969, 164 p., 21x24,5 [Denoel]
043-571-9A 45,00

Le golf. 1974, 96 p., ill., 12x20 [B M]
370-151-3B 9,90

Le golf. BERNARD, Alain – 128 p., 11,5x17,6 [P.U.F.] *(Q.S.J. No.1385)*
222-811-2B 6,90

Athlétisme pour tous. BOBIN, Robert – 6 ed., 184 p., ill., [Amphora] *(Sports)*
208-765-8B 22,80

Entraînement athlétique. DEMEILLES, Lucien – 5 ed., 240 p., ill. [Amphora] *(Sports)*
208-772-4B 22,80

Exercices éducatifs en athlétisme. *(en 2 vols.)* VANDEN EYNDE, E. – 1956, ill., 18x12 [Vander Oyez] *(Olympia No.6)*
098-588-7B

Principes de mécanique en athlétisme. DYSON, Geoffrey, H.G. – – Traduit de l'Anglais. 1971, 2 ed., 240 p., ill., 14x21,5 [Vigot]
278-158-1B 55,00

Condition physique du sportif et de l'homme moderne. DELORE, Michel – 1975, 196 p., 16x24 [Amphora]
405-671-9B 33,50

Conférences de Strasbourg. [Française, Féd. ed. phy. gym.]
403-769-3B 35,00

Dictionnaire de la culture physique. ROUET, Marcel – 1975, 304 p., ill., 14x21 [Casterman]
406-395-4A 65,00

Disque. Bibliographie, 24 p., [Québec Off.]
400-902-3B C$ .40

La documentation... demain. BOUTHILLETTE, Jean – Semaine de l'éducation physique. Sherbrooke, 11 au 15 novembre 1974. 1974, 14 p., ill., [Sherbrooke, lib. univ. de]
411-880-8A C$ 1,60

Les Echassier sportifs. Sylvain Dornon (Paris Moscou 1891) et les concours de l'Ascension (1892-93-94-95). RAGOT, Jacques – 1972. [Ragot]
442-085-7B 7,00

Education sportive et athletisme par le jeu. BOBIN, Robert – 1976, 441-049-4B 38,10

Emile Jacques-Dalcroze. L'homme, le compositeur, le créateur de la rythmique. MARTIN, Frank – 1965, 596 p., ill., 15x21,5 [Baconnière]
425-218-5A FS 44,00
425-218-5B FS 36,00

L'éveil sportif. LE BOEUF, – 1975, [Ecole]
404-567-0B 35,00

Le grand livre de l'athlétisme. MEYER, Gaston – 1975, 320 p., ill., 21x24 [Calmann-Lévy]
412-669-4B 110,00

Haltérophilie. Bibliographie, 24 p., [Québec Off.]
400-927-0B C$ .40

Hauteur. Bibliographie, 24 p., [Québec Off.]
400-905-6B C$ .40

Hebertisme et médecine. [Française, Féd. ed phy. gym.]
403-764-4B 3,00

Javelot. Bibliographie, 24 p., [Québec Off.] 400-904-9B C$ .40

Longueur. Bibliographie, 24 p., [Québec Off.] 400-906-4B C$ .40

Marteau. Bibliographie, 24 p., [Québec Off.] 400-903-1B C$ .40

Mémento d'entraînement physique. BARNIER, Lucien – PODEVIN, A. – [France-Sélection]
403-825-3B 21,00

Cours de l'école de yoga de Montreux. 6 disques, 14 leçons— [Vie et action]
440-004-0B 350,00

Cours pratiques de yoga. ANTONI, Charles – [Paris, productions de]
404-930-0B 9,50

Cours simplifié et pratique de Raja Yoga. SLATER, Wallace – 1970, 170 p., 11,4x17,8 [Adyar]
209-772-3B 14,00

Culture physique. DEBUIGNE, Gérard – 5 ed., 164 p., ill., [Amphora] *(Sports)*
208-768-2B 18,75

La culture physique athlétique. ROUET, Marcel – ill., in-16 [Bornemann] *(Sportive)*
048-286-9B 6,00

La Culture virile par l'action physique. HEBERT, Georges – 1946, 5 ed., [Vuibert]
092-502-4B 3,50

L'éducation dans les écoles normales du Québec, 1836. 1969. GUAY, Donald – 1969, 96 p., [Sports-Loisirs]
165-974-7A C$ 2,25

Education physique et milieu du travail. BEKAERT, Antoine – BOSQUET, F. – 1962, 18x12 [Vander Oyez]
098-378-3B 10,80

L'éducation physique ou l'entraînement complet par la méthode naturelle. Historique. HEBERT, Georges – 1947, 12 ed., [Vuibert]
092-491-0B 8,00

Education physique pour tous. CLERC, Pierre – CRENN, Roger – LISTELLO, Auguste – 4 ed., 300 p. ill. [Amphora] *(Sports)*
208-771-6B 28,95

L'éducation physique, virile et morale par la Méthode naturelle. – 2. Technologie. Marche. Course. Saut. HEBERT, Georges – 1949, 3 ed., [Vuibert]
092-492-8B 12,50

L'éducation physique, virile et morale par la Méthode naturelle. – 3.1. Quad– dile. HEBERT, Georges – 1946, 2 ed., [Vuibert]
092-493-6B 12,50

L'éducation physique, virile et morale par la Méthode naturelle. – 3.2. Grimper. HEBERT, Georges – 1947, 2 ed., [Vuibert]
092-194-4B 12,50

L'éducation physique, virile et morale par la Méthode naturelle. – 3.3. Equilibrisme. HEBERT, Georges – 1958, 2 ed., [Vuibert]
092-495-1B 12,50

L'éducation physique, virile et morale par la Méthode naturelle. – 4.1. Lever. HEBERT, Georges – [Vuibert]
092-496-9B 12,50

L'éducation physique, virile et morale par la Méthode naturelle. – 4.2. Lancer. HEBERT, Georges – 1950. [Vuibert]
092-497-7B 16,00

L'éducation physique, virile et morale par la Méthode naturelle. – 4.3. Défense. HEBERT, Georges – 1955. [Vuibert]
092-498-5E 16,00

L'éducation physique, virile et morale par la Méthode naturelle. – 5. Natation. HEBERT, Georges – 1959. [Vuibert]
092-499-3B 39,00

En pleine forme. GAGNON, Alphonse – 160 p., [Jour] *(Petite collection No.4)*
249-057-1B C$ 1,50

125

7-107

Plate 15

00-07 Books. Bibliography. Libraries.
General works and miscellanies

00 Book production and trade. Bibliophily

g Trömel, Ferdinand: Das Buch- und Presse-
   wesen im .alten Husum. Mit einer Husum-
   Bibliographie. Husum. Husum Druck- und
   Verlagsgesellschaft. 1975. 47 p. ill. 00.09
g Laxness, Halldór: Verlagslunch in Kopenha-
   gen. (Halldór Laxness: Zeit zu schreiben. Mün-
   chen. p. 181–184). 00.4

01 Bibliography

01.2 Bibliographies of specific authors

b Baeva, Magdalena & Elena Furnadžieva: Chans
   Kristian Andersen. Bio-bibliografski očerk.
   Sofija. Dom na literaturata i izkustvata za deca
   i junoši. 1975. 63 p. ill. 01.2
e Lerche, Grith: A bibliography of the works of
   Axel Steensberg 1936–1976. (Axel Steensberg.
   Cph. p. 52–88, ill.). 01.2
f L'Hoest, Christian: Essai de bibliographie des
   traductions françaises de Hans-Christian Andersen (1840–1976). Bruxelles. Ambassade du
   Danemark. 87 p. 01.2
r Pereslegina, E. V.: Otto Gel'sted. Biobibliogra-
   fičeskij ukazatel'. Moskva. Kniga. 43 p. 01.2

01.36 Bibliographies of specific institutions,
Denmark

e Theses and other publications of the University
   of Copenhagen 1975. Cph. IDÉ. 8 p. 01.36

01.56 National bibliography, Denmark

e Dania polyglotta. Literature on Denmark in languages other than Danish & books of Danish
   interest published abroad. Comp. by the Danish Department of the Royal Library. Ed. by
   Jan William Rasmussen, Sven C. Jacobsen,
   Karsten Kromann. New series 7, 1975. Cph.
   The Royal Library. 109 p. 01.56
e The Danish national bibliography: Serials. Supplement 1970/75. Comp. by the Danish Department of the Royal Library. Cph. The Danish Library Bureau. 136 p. 01.56

01.6 Special bibliography

v Skov, H. C.: Danish book-plate literature. [e,
   g]. Frederikshavn. Exlibristen. 137 p. ill.
   01.6009
s Schwarz, David: Invandrar- och minoritetsfrå-
   gor. Nordisk bibliografi. Sthlm. Stockholms
   Universitet. 105 p. 01.63016
e Aareskjold, Helen V.: Bibliography of Scandinavian political science for 1974 and 1975.
   = Scandinavian political studies. Oslo. Vol. 11,
   p. 189–236. 01.632
s Schwarz, David: Invandrar- och minoritetsfrå-
   gor. Nordisk bibliografi. Sthlm. Stockholms
   Universitet. 105 p. 01.6326
e Friedman, Philip S.: A Danish-American bibliography. = Scandinavian studies. Lawrence,
   Kan. Vol. 48, p. 441–444. 01.63261
e Søndergaard, Jens: Danish legal publication in
   English, French and German. 1963–74. Sthlm.
   Almqvist & Wiksell. p. 267–337. 01.634
e Skaar, Finn Erik: Papers on the stratigra-
   phy of Greenland. (Finn Erik Skaar: Recent
   scientific investigations and literature. Oslo.
   1973. p. 29–31). 01.6554
e The Danish national bibliography: Music.
   1972/73. Comp. by the Music Department of
   the Royal Library. Ed. by Annette Laursen.
   Ballerup. The Danish Library Bureau. 83 p.
   01.6783
e The Danish national bibliography: Music. 1975.
   Comp. by the Music Department of the Royal
   Library. Ed. by Susanne Sugar. Ballerup. The
   Danish Library Bureau. 55 p. 01.6783
e Ober, Kenneth H.: Contributions in Dutch,
   English, Faroese, German, Icelandic, Italian
   and Slavic languages to Danish literary history
   1925–1970. A provisional bibliography. Kbh.
   Det kongelige Bibliotek. 32 p. 01.6816
f L'Hoest, Christian: Essai de bibliographie des
   traductions françaises de Hans-Christian Andersen (1840–1976). Bruxelles. Ambassade du Danemark. 87 p. 01.6869
e List of books and articles published by Scandinavian Slavists and Baltologists 1975–76. =
   Scando-slavica, tom. 22, p. 205–212. 01.690
e Contributions to Scandinavian studies in other
   periodicals. = Scandinavica. London. Vol. 15,
   p. 85–99. 01.695
e Select bibliography of contributions to economic and social history appearing in Scandinavian books, periodicals and year-books, 1975.
   By Per Boje a. o. = Scand econ hist rev, vol.
   24, p. 174–184. 01.695

Plate 16

70 Psycho-physical method. (W. McDougall.) (*In* Lectures on the method of science. Edited by T. B. Strong. Oxford University Press, 1906. Pp. 110-131.)

71 The case of Sally Beauchamp. By W. McDougall. (*In* Proceedings of the society for psychical research, 1907, 19, 410-431.)

See Morton Prince's *The Dissociation of a Personality: A Biographical Study in Abnormal Psychology* (London, 1906). "Sally" was one of three distinct personalities coexistent in Miss Beauchamp.

72 A practicable eugenic suggestion. By W. McDougall. Read before a meeting of the sociological society (at the school of economics and political science, University of London), on Feb. 21, 1906, Dr. F. W. Mott in the chair. (*In* Sociological papers, Vol. III, published for the sociological society. London: Macmillan and Co., Ltd., 1907. Pp. 55-80.)

72a Discussion on the above, by C. W. Saleeby, Benjamin Kidd, Mr. Darbisher, L. N. G. Filon, and F. W. Mott. *Written communications* on the same, by Mr. Elderton, Francis Galton, Archdall Reid, E. H. J. Schuster, and J. L. Taylor. (*Ibid.*, III, 81-99.)

72b Mr. McDougall's reply. (*Ibid.*, III, 99-104.)

73 Review of *The integrative action of the nervous system.* By C. S. Sherrington. London, 1906. (*In* Brain, 1907, 30, 376-392.)

74 Fatigue. By William McDougall. (*In* Report of the seventy-eighth meeting of the British association, Dublin, Sept., 1908. London, 1909. Pp. 479-489.)

Ordered by the General Committee (of the Association) to be printed *in extenso.*

75 An investigation of the colour sense of two infants. By William McDougall. (*In* The British journal of psychology, 1908, 2, 338-352.)

76 With HOCART, A. M. Some data for a theory of auditory perception of direction. By A. M. Hocart and

[21]

Plate 17

127

1. ABADIE, M.C.

   1953. — Inventaire des espèces fruitières comestibles à Madagascar.
   Bulletin de l'Académie Malgache, Tananarive, n° 30, 1953, pp. 185-203.

   Environ 125 espèces, groupées en 92 familles, sont décrites : noms scien-
   tifiques, noms vernaculaires (français et indigènes), période de fructifica-
   tion, régions et altitudes auxquelles l'espèce se développe, abondance
   relative et remarques.

2. ABELING, E.J., BEACHELL, H.M., BRADSHAW, C.A., COTTON, R.T.
   and alii.

   1959. — The Chemistry and Technology of Cereals as Food and Feed.
   AVI, Westport, Connecticut, 1959, 1 vol., 732 p.

   Plusieurs auteurs ont collaboré à la rédaction de cet ouvrage où, dans
   la première partie, ils définissent quelques céréales grainières : froment,
   maïs, avoine, orge, seigle, sorgho, riz, mil, Zizania aquatica, Oryzopsis
   hymenoides et Coix lacryma-jobi.

   Dans la deuxième partie, ils traitent des méthodes de transformation :
   meunerie, production de macaroni, production d'huiles, préparation d'ali-
   ments pour le bétail, etc.

   Enfin, dans une troisième partie, ils passent en revue les caractéristiques
   fonctionnelles et d'emmagasinage des produits : détérioration de la saveur
   des produits dus à la transformation des lipides, suffisance des céréales dans
   l'alimentation humaine, leur rôle dans l'alimentation du bétail, effets et
   détection des insectes et des rongeurs.

3. (...

   1951. — Abstracts of Some Articles Pertaining to the Cultivation of
   Black Pepper.

   Technical Collaboration Branch, Office of Foreign Agricultural Relations. United States Department of Agriculture, Washington, January
   1951, 1 vol., 45 p., tabl., graph., ill., bibl.

   Cette note est constituée d'une série d'articles résumés concernant le
   poivre noir et plus particulièrement la biologie florale, le sol, la reproduction, les pratiques culturales et la technologie.

4. ACENA, B. and PUNO, G.D.

   1955. — A Study on the Use of Cassava in the Beer Industry.
   The Philippine Journal of Agriculture, Manila, vol. XX, n°ˢ 1-2, 1955,
   pp. 1-13, tabl., graph., bibl.

   Le goût de la bière de cassave est comparable à celui d'autres bières com-
   merciales. L'amidon de cassave est le plus indiqué pour servir de produit
   d'adjonction au brassage. Le raccourcissement de la durée de saccharification
   diminue le prix de revient. La cassave se caractérise par un forte teneur en
   extraits, un faible taux d'eau et d'huile ; sa farine peut également être utilisée.

— 1 —

Plate 18

ECONOMIC AND SOCIAL HISTORY

ECONOMIC

General

ANON. How governmental restraint of Irish trade with America during 537
our war for independence affected England's 'sister kingdom and
island'. From a summary of European history published in a London periodical in the year 1779. *J. am. Hist.*, xxiii (1929) 26-29.

——. The English industrial revolution of the eighteenth century. *Edin-* 538
burgh R., ccv (1907) 125-43. [Review of no. 567.]

BOWDEN (WITT). Industrial society in England towards the end of the 539
eighteenth century. New York, 1925. xiii, 343 pp., bibliog. [*Rev. Am.*
hist. R., xxx (1925) 808-09; E.H.R., xli (1926) 606-08; T.L.S. (1925)
289-90.]

BRISCO (NORRIS ARTHUR). The economic policy of Robert Walpole. (Colum- 540
bia University. Studies in History, Economics and Public Law. 27, i). New
York, 1907. 222 pp. [*Rev. R.* hist., cii (1909) 165.]

CHAMBERS (JONATHAN DAVID). Nottinghamshire in the eighteenth 541
century: a study of life and labour under the squirearchy. 1932. xi, 377 pp.,
maps + *errata* and *addenda* slip. [*Rev.* Ec.H.R., iv (1934) 365-67; E.H.R.,
xlviii (1933) 716-17; T.L.S. (1932) 551.]

CROSS (ARTHUR LYON) ed. Eighteenth-century documents relating to the 542
royal forests, the sheriffs and smuggling. Selected from the Shelburne
manuscripts in the William L. Clements Library. (Univ. of Michigan
Pubns. History and Political Science. 7). New York, 1928. xvii, 328 pp.,
front., fac. [*Rev.* Am. hist. R., xxxiv (1929) 119-20; E.H.R., xliv (1929)
498-99; History, xv (1931) 190-91.]

CUNNINGHAM (WILLIAM). The rise and decline of the free trade move- 543
ment. 1904. x, 168 pp. [*Rev.* Am. hist. R., xiv (1909) 138-40; T.L.S. (1904)
375.]

DOWDELL (ERIC GEORGE). The economic administration of Middlesex 544
from the accession of Charles II to the death of George II studied in the
records of quarter sessions. *Univ. Oxford Abstracts Diss. D.Phil.*, ii (1929)
37-55.

FAY (CHARLES RYLE). The corn laws and social England. Cambridge, 1932. 545
xii, 223 pp. [*Rev.* Am. hist. R., xxxviii (1933) 794; T.L.S. (1933) 69.]

——. Two Empires. Cambridge, 1928. 24 pp. [*Rev.* T.L.S. (1928) 495.] 546
Cf. no. 547.

53

Plate 19

129

ETHNOGRAPHY

I. GENERAL WORKS AND COMPARATIVE STUDIES

(a) JOURNALS

The principal journals dealing with South African ethnography are:

1. AFRICA. 1928– . Published quarterly by the Oxford University Press for the International Institute of African Languages and Cultures.

2. BANTU STUDIES. 1921– . Published quarterly by the University of the Witwatersrand Press, Johannesburg.

3. NADA. 1923– . Published annually by the Native Affairs Department of the Southern Rhodesia Government.

4. REPORT OF THE SOUTH AFRICAN ASSOCIATION FOR THE ADVANCEMENT OF SCIENCE, 1903–8; continued as SOUTH AFRICAN JOURNAL OF SCIENCE, 1909– . Published annually by the South African Association for the Advancement of Science, Johannesburg.

(b) BIBLIOGRAPHIES

(i) Periodical

5. AFRICA. From vol. 2 (1929) onwards publishes quarterly lists of recent works on African (including S. African) ethnography.

6. ETHNOLOGISCHER ANZEIGER. 1928– . Published at irregular intervals by E. Schweizerbart'schc Verlagsbuchhandlung, Stuttgart.

Each volume contains a special section listing recent works on S. Africa.

7. JOURNAL DE LA SOCIÉTÉ DES AFRICANISTES. 1931– . Published semi-annually by the Société des Africanistes, Paris.

Each volume contains a lengthy list of recent ethnographical publications on S. Africa.

(ii) Special

8. HAMBLY, W. D. 1937. Source Book for African Anthropology. Chicago: Field Museum of Natural History, *Anthropological Series*, vol. **36**. 2 vols. Pp. 953.

Bibliography of authors, 733–835; special index for S. Africa, 838; list of bibliographies, 849–52.

9. LEWIN, E. 1930. Subject Catalogue of the Library of the Royal Empire Society. London: The Royal Empire Society. 3 vols. Vol. I: The British Empire generally, and Africa. Pp. x+139*+582+cxxiii.

Ethnography of S. Africa generally, 354–61; Southern Rhodesia, 245–6; Bechuanaland, 444; Basutoland, 446; South-West Africa, 453. Useful for non-technical periodical literature.

Plate 20

INDEX